DAILY STRENGTH
for the BATTLE

DAILY STRENGTH
for the BATTLE

A SPIRITUAL WARFARE
PROMISE BOOK

Compiled by
BETH NETHERY FEIA

VINE
BOOKS

SERVANT PUBLICATIONS
ANN ARBOR, MICHIGAN

Vine Books is an imprint of Servant Publications especially designed to serve evangelical Christians.

Published by Servant Publications
P.O. Box 8617
Ann Arbor, Michigan 48107

Printed in the United States of America
ISBN 1-56955-148-0

CONTENTS

PROMISES OF FREEDOM AND PROTECTION

PROMISES FOR RELEASE FROM BONDAGE

PROMISES FOR SAFETY
THROUGH SPIRITUAL ARMOR

PROMISES THAT CAN
SET OTHERS FREE

PROMISES FOR PEOPLE WE LOVE AND PLACES IN WHICH WE LIVE

PROMISES FOR CHANGING OUR WORLD

For you created my inmost being; you knit me together in my mother's womb. I praise you because I am fearfully and wonderfully made; your works are wonderful, I know that full well. PSALM 139:13-14

Praise be to the God and Father of our Lord Jesus Christ, who has blessed us in the heavenly realms with every spiritual blessing in Christ. For he chose us in him before the creation of the world to be holy and blameless in his sight. In love he predestined us to be adopted as his sons through Jesus Christ. EPHESIANS 1:3-5

Do You Know Who You Really Are?

Our enemy is opposed to our discovering who we are. Indeed, he is greatly threatened by us and the position God has given us. Since his primary concern is to enhance his own position in the universe, it is to be expected that he is jealous of us. For we (not he) are in second place in the universe. Only we (not he or any other creature) are created in God's image. Though both Satan and humans rebelled, only humans have been redeemed from their rebellion. Was redemption offered to Satan and his followers? We do not know. If it was, Satan's kingdom has rejected it.

What we do know, though, is that any human being who trusts Jesus Christ is restored to the relationship with

God for which we were created. We again become members of God's family. This makes our enemy jealous and anxious to do all he can to keep believers from discovering who they really are. He, of course, doesn't want us to discover who God is. But *he is equally afraid we'll discover who we are.* He is jealous of the attention God showers on his children and the position he gives them. Satanic beings counter by spying out our weaknesses and exploiting them to the fullest, especially in areas where God has given us something they don't possess.

He especially targets the godlike characteristics God has built into us. For example, only we are in God's image. So Satan works hard to cripple our self-image. Only we and God can create new beings who are in God's image. So Satan attacks our sexuality. Only we and God can relate to others at a deep spiritual level. So he attacks human relationships, especially between family members, but also any other close relationships that are vulnerable.

You have been chosen by God, made in his image, redeemed by his love, and treasured as his child. All of his riches and power are yours.

How great is the love the Father has lavished on us, that we should be called children of God! And that is what we are!

1 JOHN 3:1

Those who are led by the Spirit of God are sons of God. For you did not receive a spirit that makes you a slave again to fear, but you received the Spirit of sonship. And by him we cry, "Abba, Father." The Spirit himself testifies with our spirit that we are God's children. Now if we are children, then we are heirs—heirs of God and co-heirs with Christ.

ROMANS 8:14-17

Adopted Into the Family of the King

These verses assure us we are *special* to God. For me, it has taken a long time to accept this as truth and to stop arguing with God about who I am. His Word and his behavior toward us can be trusted. So now I like to ask discouraged Christians, "Do you know who you really are?" People usually answer such things as "a Christian," "a believer," and "redeemed." Those answers are, of course, true. And each is precious. But, to me, the most precious of all the claims we can make about our relationship with God is that he has adopted us as his *children*, his own sons and daughters.

We are fashioned in God's image—something that cannot be said of any other being. Then, when we fell, God redeemed us, forgave us, and replaced our sin nature so that "God's very nature is in [us]; and because God is [our] Father, [we] cannot continue to sin" (1 Jn 3:9).

This position endows us, then, with both the authority and the inheritance that belong to members of God's family. *Think of it, we have been adopted right into the family of the King of the whole universe!*

As God's beloved child, you now share his holy nature. You are no longer a slave to sin. You are free.

Therefore, there is now no condemnation for those who are in Christ Jesus.   ROMANS 8:1

Once you were alienated from God and were enemies in your minds because of your evil behavior. But now he has reconciled you by Christ's physical body through death to present you holy in his sight, without blemish and free from accusation.   COLOSSIANS 1:21-22

God Wants to Shower You With Love and Acceptance

Many of us live our days constantly falling short of our standards and feeling we are unacceptable to ourselves, others, and God. We really want to believe God loves us. We want to take our place as a "prince" or "princess" in his kingdom. We want to believe in the tremendous power available for us as his children. But our self-condemnation keeps us from accepting what is rightfully our inheritance.

I personally have struggled with this problem. For years, I had a "negative tape" inside my head continually playing the enemy's lies. He said things like, "Reject yourself; you're no good," "You are a no-good, failure-prone sinner and will never be anything else," "Carry your guilt; your sins are too great for even God to forgive," "See how unworthy and inadequate you are; you're always messing things up," "Worry about what others think of you," "Fear that you're going to fail again," and so on. In short, those messages were telling me I was unacceptable and unworthy to be the prince or princess God has adopted me to be.

By opening up to God's truth and utilizing his healing power, however, I am being "reprogrammed" by Jesus and am learning from him to receive his acceptance and love. The "tape" he plays in my mind conveys quite different messages, true messages. He says to me, "Because I have accepted you as you are, you can accept yourself," "I love and accept you for who you are, not for what you do," "You are forgiven, and you don't need to feel guilty anymore," "I chose you; don't argue with my choice," "I have made you worthy and adequate," "I will never leave you nor forsake you," "Don't fear; cast all your cares on me, for I care for you," and so on.

He wants you to hear him saying the same things to you. His desire is that you truly understand, deep within, his love for you and your place in his kingdom.

The King of the universe thinks enough of
you to grant you far more love and
acceptance than you
ordinarily grant yourself.

Therefore, if anyone is in Christ, he is a new creation; the old has gone, the new has come!   2 CORINTHIANS 5:17

May God himself, the God of peace, sanctify you through and through. May your whole spirit, soul and body be kept blameless at the coming of our Lord Jesus Christ. The one who calls you is faithful and he will do it.
1 THESSALONIANS 5:23-24

Why We Struggle to Accept Our Inheritance

In his book *The Seven Gifts*, Bernard Kelly uses a powerful analogy to help us understand the difficulty Christians have in accepting their inheritance. Kelly likens this struggle to a slum child adopted by a royal family. At first, the slum child rejoices that he is out of the slum and living in a palace. The child's new father, the king, tells the slum child he no longer needs to live in the dark, hateful streets where he once lived. Furthermore, the king tells his new son that all of the royal family treasures now belong to him as their adopted child. In spite of this joyful inheritance, the child remembers the way people in the slum treated him and the abuse he suffered. Something within him cries out, "It can't be true!"

Unfortunately, this poor slum child has brought much "slum baggage" with him to his new palace. The royal family could take him out of the slum, but getting the slum out of him is another matter. Fortunately, his new loving parents understand this, "take his hand," and teach him to trust their unconditional love. Caringly, patiently, they help him along until he can truly acknowledge and accept his new life and inheritance.*

Many Christians react exactly like that slum child. They have been given a new life and inheritance as children of the Most High King! Like the slum child, they too bring their baggage of hurts and wounds. We have internal tapes that cry out, "It can't be true!" Here we need to give the Holy Spirit our hands and seek healing of the wounds that block acceptance of our rightful inheritance. Jesus desires that our stumbling blocks—our self-hatred, our fears, our unworthiness—be removed. He wants to help us step forward to claim our rightful place as his children.

> *When doubts cloud your mind, when you are tempted to believe, "It can't be true," reach up and take your Father's hand. Hear his voice say, "I love you with an everlasting love. All the joy, strength, and riches you need, I delight to give to you."*

* Bernard Kelly, *The Seven Gifts* (London: Sheed and Ward, 1941), 12–14.

Philip said, "Lord, show us the Father and that will be enough for us." Jesus answered: "Don't you know me, Philip, even after I have been among you such a long time? Anyone who has seen me has seen the Father." JOHN 14:8-9

As a father has compassion on his children, so the Lord has compassion on those who fear him; for he knows how we are formed, he remembers that we are dust. PSALM 103:13-14

A True Picture of Our Heavenly Father

When we give ourselves to Christ, we are adopted by a heavenly Father in whose presence we are welcome at any time. Many of us, however, struggle with the reality of a heavenly Father who unconditionally loves and accepts us. The reason may be that we have not experienced such love and acceptance from our earthly fathers. Many of us have endured neglect and even abuse from our fathers and can't imagine any other kind of treatment from someone called "father."

I have ministered to a number of people whose concept of "father" had been damaged in major ways. One woman's definition of father had become, "Someone who always stands in my way whenever I really want to do something." Another's came out in the statement, "Whenever I picture Jesus, I always see him with a stick in his hand."

Such people usually find that at the deepest level they cannot accept the truth that God is not like their earthly fathers—even though they have accepted that truth on a rational level.

Another problem for many people is their anger at God for allowing bad things to happen to them. They have been taught that God can do anything he wants. When they experience difficulty, they reason, it must be because God doesn't care enough about them to protect them. So they are angry at God and convinced he endorses their low opinion of themselves.

Such false perceptions of our heavenly Father provide some of the greatest blocks to understanding and functioning in our spiritual authority. Faulty pictures of the Father or of Jesus need to be corrected before we can take our rightful places as God's princes and princesses. We must renounce and refuse to listen any longer to the lies we've been hearing about our Father.

Picture the best father you can imagine.
Your heavenly Father exceeds your fondest
hopes. He loves you perfectly, cares
for you intimately, and is worthy
of your complete trust.

Praise be to the God and Father of our Lord Jesus Christ, who has blessed us in the heavenly realms with every spiritual blessing in Christ. For he chose us in him before the creation of the world to be holy and blameless in his sight. In love he predestined us to be adopted as his sons through Jesus Christ.

EPHESIANS 1:3-5

Take Your Self-Estimate From God

Develop the picture of your worth and value from God, not from the false reflections that come out of your past. The healing of low self-esteem really hinges on a choice you must make: Will you listen to Satan as he employs all the lies, the distortions, the put-downs, and the hurts of your past to keep you bound by unhealthy, unchristian feelings and concepts about yourself? Or will you receive your self-esteem from God and His Word?

Here are some very important questions to ask yourself.

- What right have you to belittle or despise someone God *loves* so deeply? Don't say, "Well, I know God loves me, but I just can't stand myself." That's a travesty of faith, an insult to God. You are failing to realize how much God loves you and how much you mean to him.

- What right have you to belittle or despise someone God has *honored* so highly? "Consider the incredible love that the Father has shown us in allowing us to be called 'children of God'" (1 Jn 3:1, PHILLIPS). And that's not just what we're called. It's what we are.

- What right have you to belittle or despise someone God *values* so highly? You are someone God values so highly that he gave the life of his own dear Son to redeem you.

- What right have you to belittle or despise someone God has *provided* for so fully? "How much more shall your Father which is in heaven give good things?" (Mt 7:11). "God shall supply all your needs" (Phil 4:19). This doesn't sound as if he wants you to be self-loathing or to feel inadequate.

- What right have you to belittle or despise someone in whom God *delights*? The apostle Paul said that we are "accepted in the beloved" (Eph 1:6). Do you remember the Father's words at the baptism of Jesus? "This is my Son, whom I love; with him I am well pleased" (Mt 3:17). Paul gives us a daring thought: we are "in Christ." God looks at you in Christ and says to you, "You are My beloved son, you are My beloved daughter, in whom I am well pleased."

From where will you get your idea of yourself? Will you say, "No, I will not listen to those lies from the past any longer. I am going to listen to God's opinion of me and let him reprogram me until his loving estimate of me becomes a part of my life, right down to my innermost feelings."

Lift your head high. God loves you.
He delights in you. He values you.

21

We demolish arguments and every pretension that sets itself up against the knowledge of God, and we take captive every thought to make it obedient to Christ.

2 CORINTHIANS 10:5

Exchanging Satan's Lies for God's Truth

Ask God to help you spot Satan's lies each time they come up in your thoughts. Speak these truths out loud. Declare, in Jesus' name, that you are not going to believe Satan's lies anymore.

1. *Satan's lie:* God can't love me.
   God's truth: "The Lord is ... loving toward all he has made" (Ps 145:13b).

2. *Satan's lie:* I am worthless.
   God's truth: "Your body is a temple of the Holy Spirit, who is in you.... You were bought at a price" (1 Cor 6:19-20).

3. *Satan's lie:* Sin will always get the better of me.
   God's truth: "No, in all these things we are more than conquerors through him who loved us" (Rom 8:37).

4. *Satan's lie:* God can't be trusted.
   God's truth: "The Lord is good, a refuge in times of trouble. He cares for those who trust in him" (Na 1:7).

5. *Satan's lie:* I don't need God.
   God's truth: "Do not hold against us the sins of the fathers; may your mercy come quickly to meet us, for we are in desperate need" (Ps 79:8).

6. *Satan's lie:* God will always keep me guessing.
   God's truth: "Trust in the Lord with all your heart and lean not on your own understanding; in all your ways acknowledge him, and he will make your paths straight" (Prv 3:5-6).

7. *Satan's lie:* Sin and darkness offer relief, while righteousness demands impossible perfection.
   God's truth: "Everyone who sins is a slave to sin" (Jn 8:34); "The wages of sin is death" (Rom 6:23); "The fruit of righteousness will be peace" (Is 32:17).

8. *Satan's lie:* God's secret purpose is to punish me.
   God's truth: "Delight yourself in the Lord and he will give you the desires of your heart" (Ps 37:4); "'I know the plans I have for you,' declares the Lord, 'plans to prosper you and not to harm you, plans to give you hope and a future'" (Jer 29:11).

9. *Satan's lie:* God expects me to be what I can't be.
   God's truth: "For it is by grace you have been saved, through faith—and this not from yourselves, it is the gift of God" (Eph 2:8).

10. *Satan's lie:* God isn't interested in my comfort. He only wants people who sacrifice themselves.
    God's truth: "For I desire mercy, not sacrifice, and acknowledgment of God rather than burnt offerings" (Hos 6:6).

*When you take hold of God's truth,
Satan's lies no longer have
power over you.*

The mind controlled by the Spirit is life and peace.

ROMANS 8:6

Your word, O Lord, is eternal; it stands firm in the heavens.

PSALM 119:89

I have hidden your word in my heart that I might not sin against you. PSALM 119:11

Let the word of Christ dwell in you richly.

COLOSSIANS 3:16

Establishing God's Word in Our Minds

We need to establish God's Word in our minds as a replacement for Satan's falsehoods.

Let's look at some of the truths about God's plan for us.

1. I am a child of God. (Rom 8:15-16; Gal 3:26; 4:6)

2. I am no longer condemned. (Rom 8:1)

3. I am an heir to God's kingdom. (Gal 3:26; Rom 8:17; Jn 1:12; Ti 3:7)

4. I am a member of the kingdom. (Gal 3:29)

5. I am light. (Mt 5:14)

6. I am salt. (Mt 5:13)

7. I am chosen. (Eph 1:4; Jn 15:16)

8. I am a dwelling place of God. (1 Cor 3:16; 6:19)

9. I am a member of the holy priesthood. (1 Pt 2:4-5)

10. I am a citizen of the kingdom of God and therefore have rights. (Phil 3:20)

11. I am forgiven. (Eph 1:7)

12. I am gifted. (Rom 12:6)

13. I assume a strategic position in the kingdom. (Rom 12:5)

14. I am called. (Eph 4:1)

15. I am a friend of Christ. (Jn 15:14)

16. I have already passed from death to life. (Jn 5:24)

17. I am holy and blameless. (Eph 1:4)

18. I am God's workmanship. (Eph 2:10)

Know that God has a beautiful plan for
you as his child, one that invites
full participation in his glory.

Put on the full armor of God so that you can take your stand against the devil's schemes. For our struggle is not against flesh and blood, but against the rulers, against the authorities, against the powers of this dark world and against the spiritual forces of evil in the heavenly realms.

EPHESIANS 6:11-12

The reason the Son of God appeared was to destroy the devil's work. 1 JOHN 3:8

You, dear children, are from God and have overcome them, because the one who is in you is greater than the one who is in the world. 1 JOHN 4:4

God's Power Is Far Greater Than the Enemy's

Satan asserts his authority over the earth when he says to Jesus, "I will give you all this power and all this wealth.... It has all been handed over to me, and I can give it to anyone I choose" (Lk 4:6). He is referred to by Jesus as "the prince of this world" (Jn 14:30); by Paul as "the ruler of the kingdom of the air" (Eph 2:2); by Peter as one who "roams around like a roaring lion, looking for someone to devour" (1 Pt 5:8); and by John as the one who rules the whole world (1 Jn 5:19).

Despite such statements concerning the impressive position of our enemy, neither Jesus nor other New Testament characters seemed alarmed by Satan's activities. They dealt with them matter-of-factly, knowing that God's power is infinitely greater than that of the enemy.

Scripture makes it clear, however, that Jesus and his followers took demons seriously. While they were not afraid of them, they acknowledged their existence and used the power of the Holy Spirit to fight them. Over and over again, references to demons and Satan's kingdom appear in the Gospels. In the Gospel of Mark, for example, over half of Jesus' ministry is devoted to delivering the demonized.

No one seemed to doubt the existence of demons or the supernatural realm in these biblical accounts. Jesus' critics questioned the source of his power (Lk 11:14-22), but, unlike those influenced by contemporary Western worldviews, they never questioned the existence of demons who indwelt and harmed people.

The Bible is clear that Satan has a powerful kingdom that Christians must reckon with at every turn. And we are living in the midst of it—in enemy territory. In Paul's day, he could state, "We know what [Satan's] plans are" (2 Cor 2:11). In our day, we need to be taught the enemy's strategy if we are to be prepared for battle.

You do not need to be intimidated by evil.
Although Satan has power, God's power is
greater still, and his power is yours.

Be self-controlled and alert. Your enemy the devil prowls around like a roaring lion looking for someone to devour. Resist him, standing firm in the faith. 1 PETER 5:8-9

We know that we are children of God, and that the whole world is under the control of the evil one. 1 JOHN 5:19

For everyone born of God has overcome the world. This is the victory that has overcome the world, even our faith.
1 JOHN 5:4

Know Your Enemy

Satanic beings are involved in every kind of disruptive human activity. They seem to have authority over places and territories, such as buildings, cities, and temples. Additionally, they appear to have authority over social organizations and groups, and influence sinful behavior such as homosexuality, drug addiction, lust, incest, rape, and murder.

The fallen angels we call demons or evil spirits seem to be the "ground level" troops, as opposed to the "cosmic level" principalities, powers, and rulers of Ephesians 6:12. These are the ones we encounter most often during spiritual warfare. Scripture tells us that demons seek people to live in (Mt 12:43-45). They apparently envy us our bodies. They have different personalities, are destructive (Mk 9:17-29), and differ in power and wickedness (Mk 5:4; Mt 12:45).

Overcome the Enemy

Satan, unlike God, is not omnipresent. He can only be in one place at a time, though he apparently can get from place to place very quickly. The other members of the hierarchy, including demons, therefore, carry out his schemes throughout the universe. In addition to their broader assignments, it is apparently the task of evil spirits to bother humans, especially Christians. Satan does not like anything God likes. He, therefore, picks on God's favorite creatures and assigns his underlings to harass us.

We can assume the primary concern of demons is to disrupt and, if possible, cripple anything or anyone that might be a threat to Satan's domination over the world. Their guns are aimed at individuals, groups, and organizations that seek to advance God's purposes. They produce "strongholds" in people's minds (2 Cor 10:4) and probably in other places as well. They attack Christian ministries and are agents of doctrinal aberrations (1 Tim 4:1). They affect health (Lk 13:11), perhaps affect weather (Lk 8:22-25), and even have "the power over death" (Heb 2:14), *though they have no power except that allowed them by God.*

When you learn how to recognize Satan's evil work and how to resist him, you will see him flee from you. Even in the midst of the battle, you already have the victory.

*Resist the devil, and he will flee from you. Come near to God,
and he will come near to you.*　　　　　　　　JAMES 4:7-8

*"The Spirit of the Lord is on me, because he has anointed me
to preach good news to the poor. He has sent me to proclaim
freedom for the prisoners and recovery of sight for the blind,
to release the oppressed, to proclaim the year of the Lord's
favor."*　　　　　　　　　　　　　　　　　LUKE 4:18-19

How the Enemy Attacks

Before we work to resist and defeat the enemy, we should consider *how* the enemy attacks and what his tactics are. For our own tactics will depend very largely on the mode of attack.

Basically, there are three forms of attack, and these can be likened in military terms to (a) a frontal assault (or from the flank), (b) a siege or blockade, and (c) an invasion and occupation.

The common experiences of temptation, whether they come directly or indirectly (that is, from the flank), are like the straightforward assault. They may be brief, after which the enemy retreats, or sustained pressure, which some call an oppression. A "bondage" is like the siege or blockade, where the enemy breaks through and surrounds an area. With a bondage, a part of our lives is brought under the enemy's control. The enemy does not possess the area, but he can prevent it from functioning properly. The third is where the enemy actually occupies a part of our lives. It is no longer under our control at all.

There are obvious limitations to these illustrations, but they may help to give us a rough idea of what the enemy is up to, and the extent of the damage he can do in our lives. The first kind of attack is, of course, commonly experienced by every Christian, and the way to deal with it is resistance. "Resist the devil, and he will flee from you."

The second kind of attack is less common. A bondage is some habit or way of life or wrong relationship which has taken hold of a person, and even a firm resistance is insufficient to shake him free from it. The way to deal with it is loosing; this normally has to be done by another Christian, who thereby "raises the siege" or helps to "relieve the blockade."

The third kind of attack or influence is even less common. Here the person is completely under the control of an evil spirit in some area of his or her life. The way to deal with it is casting out. This has to be done by other Christians who take authority over the enemy and so oust him from his position of occupation, freeing the person to serve God.

The boundary lines between these three are not always clearly defined, but discernment and discretion will be given as to how to act.

Wherever you see Satan's foothold, stand firm and cast him out. The authority of almighty God is within you. Be confident and believe.

For the accuser of our brothers, who accuses them before our God day and night, has been hurled down. They overcame him by the blood of the Lamb and by the word of their testimony. REVELATION 12:10-11

No temptation has seized you except what is common to man. And God is faithful; he will not let you be tempted beyond what you can bear. But when you are tempted, he will also provide a way out so that you can stand up under it.

1 CORINTHIANS 10:13

Take up the shield of faith, with which you can extinguish all the flaming arrows of the evil one. EPHESIANS 6:16

Don't Believe Everything You Hear

One of the most common attitudes I have discovered in Christians is a deep-seated sense of self-depreciation. I've heard them say, "I'm not important; I'm not qualified; I'm no good." I'm amazed at how many Christians are paralyzed in their witness and productivity by thoughts and feelings of inferiority and worthlessness.

Next to temptation, perhaps the most frequent and insistent attack from Satan to which we are vulnerable is accusation. By faith we have entered into an eternal relationship with the Lord Jesus Christ. As a result, we are dead to sin and alive to God, and we now sit with Christ in the heavenlies. In Christ we *are* important, we *are* qualified, and we *are* good. Satan can do absolutely nothing to alter our position in Christ and our worth to God. But he can render us virtually inoperative if he can deceive us into listening to and believing his insidious lies accusing us of being of little value to God or other people.

Satan often uses temptation and accusation as a brutal one-two punch. He comes along and says, "Why don't you try it? Everybody does it. Besides, you can get away with it. Who's going to know?" Then as soon as we fall for his tempting line, he changes his tune to accusation: "What kind of a Christian are you to do such a thing? You're a pitiful excuse for a child of God. You'll never get away with it. You might as well give up because God has already given up on you."

In Christ you have complete forgiveness.
In Christ your sins are removed as far as
the east is from the west. In Christ you
are presented blameless before the Father.

All the people were amazed and said to each other, "What is this teaching? With authority and power he gives orders to evil spirits and they come out!"　　　　　　LUKE 4:36

In fear and amazement they asked one another, "Who is this? He commands even the winds and the water, and they obey him."　　　　　　LUKE 8:25

How Demons Try to Disrupt Our Lives

A major concern of the enemy is to disrupt people's lives, especially those of Christians. He nips at our heels like an angry dog whose space has been encroached upon. Satan is referred to as "the ruler of this world" (Jn 14:30) and doesn't like it that those who belong to another King are wandering around in "his" territory, so he harasses Christians whenever and however he can.

I don't know how much power demons have over the ordinary circumstances of life. But I would wager that they do whatever God allows to disrupt our lives through influencing such things as traffic, weather, health, stress, relationships, worship, sleep, diet, and machines (especially cars and computers). I suspect, for example, that harassment was the aim of Satan when he ordered demons to manifest themselves when Jesus was teaching in the synagogue (Lk 4:33-34); that it was he who stirred up a storm while Jesus was in a boat on Lake Galilee (Lk 8:23-24);

and that he influenced the Pharisees to persecute Jesus continually. I have developed the habit of saying when things go wrong, "If this is the enemy, stop it!" It is amazing how many difficulties fade at that command.

Before you fall prey to the frustration and discouragement of your circumstances, look for ways Satan is trying to pester you. Rebuke him. Resist him. Recall who you are in Christ, and allow God to surround you with his protection and strength.

On him we have set our hope that he will continue to deliver us, as you help us by your prayers. Then many will give thanks on our behalf for the gracious favor granted us in answer to the prayers of many.   2 CORINTHIANS 1:10-11

Devote yourselves to prayer, being watchful and thankful. And pray for us, too, that God may open a door for our message, so that we may proclaim the mystery of Christ.

COLOSSIANS 4:2-3

When a strong man, fully armed, guards his own house, his possessions are safe. But when someone stronger attacks and overpowers him, he takes away the armor in which the man trusted and divides up the spoils.   LUKE 11:21-22

Prayer Brings Protection

Satan doesn't seem to harass every Christian equally. He seems to pay more attention to those who are the greatest threat to him and to those who don't have enough prayer support. Many Christians are so passive about their Christianity that they are no threat to the enemy. They may get off with very little attention from him. I even heard of a pastor who made a bargain with Satan that he would not preach against him if he didn't cause disruption in the pastor's ministry! His was certainly a "wood, hay, and stubble" ministry, destined to be destroyed when tested by fire (1 Cor 3:12, PHILLIPS). How much better to be such a threat to the enemy that he feels it worthwhile to attack us. How much better to hear our Master say to us someday, "Well done" (Lk 19:17).

Those who threaten the enemy and do not have enough prayer support also are at risk of regular and effective harassment. It is wise for us to get a number of people supporting us in prayer, especially those with gifts of intercession, before we move strongly against the enemy. We will then take territory from him and frustrate him because we will have too much prayer protection for his attacks to get through. The fact that even Jesus was harassed and that weak Christians seem to be suggests, however, that no Christians live completely free from the enemy's attention as long as they are in his territory.

When you pray and seek the prayers of others, a wall of protection springs up to surround you. God's deliverance is activated through prayer.

Then Jesus came to them and said, "All authority in heaven and on earth has been given to me." MATTHEW 28:18

I have given you authority to trample on snakes and scorpions and to overcome all the power of the enemy.
LUKE 10:19

I pray also that the eyes of your heart may be enlightened in order that you may know ... his incomparably great power for us who believe. That power is like the working of his mighty strength, which he exerted in Christ when he raised him from the dead. EPHESIANS 1:18-19

You Plus Jesus Equals Triumph

You may think that you're not mature enough to resist demonic interference in your life. You somehow imagine that the enemy is more powerful than you are. The truth is that, while in yourself you don't have the ability to resist Satan and his demons, *in Christ you do*. The Israelites looked at Goliath fearfully and said, "We can't fight him." But young David looked at Goliath and said, "Who is this uncircumcised Philistine, that he should defy the armies of the living God?" (1 Sm 17:26), then blew him away with his slingshot. The army saw Goliath in relation to themselves and trembled; David saw Goliath in relation to God and triumphed. When you encounter the spiritual enemies of your soul, remember: You plus Jesus equals a majority.

You can do all things through Christ,
who gives you strength.

We demolish arguments and every pretension that sets itself up against the knowledge of God, and we take captive every thought to make it obedient to Christ.

2 CORINTHIANS 10:5

So then, just as you received Christ Jesus as Lord, continue to live in him, rooted and built up in him, strengthened in the faith as you were taught, and overflowing with thankfulness.

COLOSSIANS 2:6

In all these things we are more than conquerors through him who loved us.

ROMANS 8:37

Just Say No

There are three ways of responding to the demonic taunts and barbs being thrown at you during your daily walk with Christ, and two of these ways are wrong.

First, the most defeated people are those who consider demonic thoughts and believe them. A subtle thought is shot into your mind: "You don't pray, read your Bible, or witness as you should. How could God love you?" That's a bald-faced lie, because God's love is unconditional. But you start thinking about your failures and agreeing that you're probably not very lovable to God. Pretty soon you're sitting in the middle of the street going nowhere.

You feel defeated simply because you have been duped

into believing that God doesn't love you or that you will never be a victorious Christian or that you are a helpless victim of the past. There is no reason why you can't get up immediately and start walking again, but you have believed a lie and you can't go anywhere.

The second response is just as unproductive. You try to argue with the demons: "I am not ugly or stupid. I am a victorious Christian." You're proud that you don't believe what they say, but they're still controlling you and setting your agenda. You're standing in the middle of the street shouting at them when you should be marching forward.

You are not to believe evil spirits, nor are you to dialogue with them. Instead, you're to ignore them. You're equipped with the armor of God; they can't touch you unless you drop your guard. With every arrow of temptation, accusation, or deception they shoot at you, simply raise the shield of faith, deflect the attack, and walk on (Col 2:6). Take every thought captive to the obedience of Christ.

*Choose truth in the face of every lie. As
you do, you will find your maturity and
freedom increasing with every step.*

For the word of the Lord is right and true; he is faithful in all he does.　　　　　　　　　　　　　　PSALM 33:4

All your words are true; all your righteous laws are eternal.　　　　　　　　　　　　　　PSALM 119:160

Sanctify them by the truth; your word is truth.　　　　　　　　　　　　　　JOHN 17:17

Then you will know the truth, and the truth will set you free.　　　　　　　　　　　　　　JOHN 8:32

Finally, brothers, whatever is true, whatever is noble, whatever is right, whatever is pure, whatever is lovely, whatever is admirable—if anything is excellent or praiseworthy—think about such things.　　　　　　　　PHILIPPIANS 4:8

Satan Is a Yappy Dog

When I was growing up on the farm, my dad, my brother, and I would visit our neighbor's farm to share produce and labor. The neighbor had a yappy little dog that scared the socks off me. When it came barking around the corner, my dad and brother stood their ground, but I ran. Guess who the dog chased! I escaped to the top of our pickup truck while the little dog yapped at me from the ground.

Everyone except me could see that the little dog had no power over me except what I gave it. Furthermore, it had no inherent power to throw me upon the pickup; it was my *belief* that put me up there. That dog controlled me by using my mind, my emotions, my will, and my muscles, all of which were motivated by fear. Finally I gathered up my courage, jumped off the pickup, and kicked a small rock at the mutt. Lo and behold, it ran!

Satan is like that yappy little dog: deceiving people into fearing him more than God. His power is in the lie. He is the father of lies (Jn 8:44) who deceives the whole world (Rv 12:9), and consequently the whole world is under the influence of the evil one (1 Jn 5:19). He can do nothing about your position in Christ, but if he can deceive you into believing his lies about you and God, you will spend a lot of time on top of the pickup truck! You don't have to outshout him or outmuscle him to be free of his influence. You simply have to *outtruth* him.

Believe, declare, and act upon the truth of God's Word, and you will thwart Satan's strategy.

His divine power has given us everything we need for life and godliness through our knowledge of him who called us by his own glory and goodness. 2 PETER 1:3

Instead, speaking the truth in love, we will in all things grow up into him who is the Head, that is, Christ,... until we all reach unity in the faith and in the knowledge of the Son of God and become mature, attaining to the whole measure of the fullness of Christ. EPHESIANS 4:15, 13

So if the Son sets you free, you will be free indeed. JOHN 8:36

God Wants You Free and Mature

Two concepts determine the victory and fruitfulness of a Christian. The first concept is *maturity*. Paul wrote: "We will in all things grow up into him who is the Head, that is, Christ,... and become mature, attaining to the whole measure of the fullness of Christ" (Eph 4:15, 13). God has given us everything we need to grow to maturity in Christ (2 Pt 1:3). But Satan is opposed to our maturity and will do anything he can to keep us from realizing who we are and what we have in Christ.

The second concept is *freedom*. Paul declared: "It is for freedom that Christ has set us free. Stand firm, then, and do not let yourselves be burdened again by a yoke of slavery" (Gal 5:1). Before we received Christ, we were slaves to sin. But because of Christ's work on the cross, sin's power over us has been broken. Satan has no right of ownership or authority over us. He is a defeated foe, but he is committed to keeping us from realizing that. He knows he can block your effectiveness as a Christian if he can deceive you into believing that you are nothing but a product of your past, subject to sin, prone to failure, and controlled by your habits. As long as he can confuse you and blind you with his dark lies, you won't be able to see that the chains which once bound you are broken. You are free in Christ, but if the devil can deceive you into believing you're not, you won't experience the freedom which is your inheritance. I don't believe in instant maturity, but I do believe in instant freedom, and I have seen thousands of people set free by the truth. Once a person is free, you would be amazed at how quickly he or she matures!

Maturity and freedom are a result of knowledge of God's truth. Speak truth to yourself, cling to it in faith, and then watch its power go to work in your life.

He withdrew by boat privately to a solitary place.... He went up into the hills by himself to pray.   MATTHEW 14:13, 23

I am the vine; you are the branches. If a man remains in me and I in him, he will bear much fruit; apart from me you can do nothing. If anyone does not remain in me, he is like a branch that is thrown away and withers; such branches are picked up, thrown into the fire and burned. If you remain in me and my words remain in you, ask whatever you wish, and it will be given you. This is to my Father's glory, that you bear much fruit, showing yourselves to be my disciples.
JOHN 15:5-8

Our Greatest Weapon Is Intimacy With Jesus

Our greatest weapon in fighting satanic influence—whether in ourselves or in others—is our intimacy with Jesus. Jesus set the example by living his life in constant closeness to the Father. He was listening to the Father at all times. Thus he could say, "I say only what the Father has instructed me to say" (Jn 8:28). He was continually watching what the Father was doing. Thus he could say, "The Son ... does only what he sees his Father doing. What the Father does, the Son also does" (Jn 5:19). He lived in absolute dependence on the Father. Thus he could say, "By myself I can do nothing; I judge only as I hear, and my judgment is just, for I seek not to please myself but him who sent me" (Jn 5:30).

Those were Jesus' day-by-day directives. To be certain his sights were lined up with those of the Father, he regularly spent time alone with the Father. Over and over again we read that Jesus withdrew "to a solitary place" (Mt 14:13) to be alone with the Father. Jesus taught us by example how to stay close to God.

Talk to God. Keep his truths always in your
mind. Be quiet before him and let him speak.
Meditate on his Word. Worship him.
You will find yourself surrounded by
his loving arms, safe from harm.

As the deer pants for streams of water, so my soul pants for you, O God. My soul thirsts for God, for the living God. When can I go and meet with God? PSALM 42:1-2

Humble yourselves, therefore, under God's mighty hand, that he may lift you up in due time. Cast all your anxiety on him because he cares for you. 1 PETER 5:6-7

"God opposes the proud but gives grace to the humble." Submit yourselves, then, to God. Resist the devil, and he will flee from you. JAMES 4:6-7

One-Two Punch: Submit Yourself to God and Resist the Devil

The old-school approach of holiness as the pathway to victorious living is so simple and straightforward. "Forsake yourself, and submit to God." That statement sounds so harsh and often is. And yet the fullness of the Father's love, when believed and received, is sufficient to heal us.

God desires to have spiritual fellowship with us. He is waiting for us to want him alone and to find satisfaction in his presence. He grieves over our busy-ness, our idolatries, our human achievements. *"He gives grace to the humble."* If we are willing to be stripped of self and come to him in consecration, change will come, his grace will bring

48

growth in Christlikeness, be it ever so seemingly slow.

Submitting ourselves—including all our hopes, fears, needs, and dreams—to an invisible, transcendent being is not easy. God may sometimes seem obscure, sometimes quiet, and oftentimes withdrawn, but I have found that such abandonment becomes easier as our trust in him deepens.

Through Jesus, God has revealed himself as a merciful, compassionate Father who always seeks our very best. As you face strongholds in your own life that sometimes seem like immovable mountains, I suggest you take an occasional walk in the woods, or along the beach, or through a park, and honestly pour out your perplexity and pain to the one who cares for you. God gives grace to the heart that is humble. Submit yourself to the Master Potter, and trust how he chooses to place you on the wheel.

*Every day, every moment, submit yourself
to God—your goals and plans, your
wounds and fears, your hopes and
dreams. In this state of humble reliance,
you will avail yourself of God's grace and
power, his healing and freedom.*

Be joyful always; pray continually; give thanks in all circumstances, for this is God's will for you in Christ Jesus.

1 THESSALONIANS 5:16

Speak to one another with psalms, hymns and spiritual songs. Sing and make music in your heart to the Lord, always giving thanks to God the Father for everything, in the name of our Lord Jesus Christ. EPHESIANS 5:19-20

Rejoice in the Lord always. I will say it again: Rejoice!

PHILIPPIANS 4:4

Stick Near to God

Spiritual growth weakens Satan's ability to work in or on a person. To grow spiritually, we need to spend time with God both alone and in fellowship. Constant listening to and conversing with God "at all times" (1 Thes 5:17)—as friend with friend, as child with Father, as wife with husband—weakens the enemy's grasp. So does worship—singing, praising, expressing love and dedication to our Lord and Savior. So does fellowship with believers. So do Bible reading and memorization. So does being joyful (Phil 4:4), filling our minds with good thoughts, and practicing Christian behavior (Phil 4:8-9).

The enemy is defeated or at least weakened when you behave as your King expects you to behave.

I have been crucified with Christ and I no longer live, but Christ lives in me. The life I live in the body, I live by faith in the Son of God, who loved me and gave himself for me.

GALATIANS 2:20

For you know that it was not with perishable things such as silver or gold that you were redeemed from the empty way of life handed down to you from your forefathers, but with the precious blood of Christ, a lamb without blemish or defect.

1 PETER 1:18-19

How great is the love the Father has lavished on us, that we should be called children of God! And that is what we are! The reason the world does not know us is that it did not know him. Dear friends, now we are children of God, and what we will be has not yet been made known. But we know that when he appears, we shall be like him, for we shall see him as he is. Everyone who has this hope in him purifies himself, just as he is pure.

1 JOHN 3:1-3

For you died, and your life is now hidden with Christ in God. When Christ, who is your life, appears, then you also will appear with him in glory.

COLOSSIANS 3:3-4

You Belong to God

The cross we are to pick up on a daily basis is not our *own* cross but *Christ's* cross. We are closely identified with his cross, however, because we have been crucified with Christ and no longer live; Christ lives in us (Gal 2:20). We are forgiven because he died in our place; we are delivered because we died with him. We are both justified and sanctified as a result of the cross.

To pick up the cross daily means to acknowledge every day that we belong to God. We have been purchased by the blood of the Lord Jesus Christ (1 Pt 1:18-19). When we pick up the cross we affirm that our identity is not based in our physical existence but in our relationship with God. We are identified as children of God (1 Jn 3:1-3) and our lives are in Christ, who is our life (Col 3:3-4).

As a result of this acknowledgment we stop trying to do our own thing in order to live daily to please our heavenly Father. We stop trying to become something we aren't, and we rest in the finished work of Christ, who made us something very special.

The cross of Christ provides forgiveness
from what you have done and deliverance
from what you were.

Teach me your way, O Lord; lead me in a straight path because of my oppressors. Do not turn me over to the desire of my foes. PSALM 27:11-12

I charge you, in the sight of God and Christ Jesus and the elect angels, to keep these instructions without partiality. 1 TIMOTHY 5:21

Healthy Fear of God

Life is dangerous. Life is a spiritual battle. And most of the time, it seems, we don't think about how we might be under the influence of dark angels—how the devil is manipulating us toward our destruction. David wrote in Psalm 27, "Teach me your way, O Lord; lead me in a straight path." Why? *"Because of my oppressors.* Do not turn me over to the desire of my foes" (Ps 27:11-12, italics mine). It really is important to walk the straight and narrow, not just because you're sure to go to hell if you don't, but because hell is sure to come knocking at your door.

In Psalm 34:7 we read that "the angel of the Lord encamps around those *who fear him,* and he delivers them" (italics mine). Don't ignore the condition! Fearing God invites his presence and the angels who accompany him. Not fearing God does just the opposite. Paul challenged the young Timothy, "I charge you, in the sight of God and Christ Jesus *and the elect angels,* to keep these instructions," —to walk the straight and narrow, because somebody is watching.

When you take God at his word and obey him, he promises to protect you, shelter you, and be your refuge from evil.

Come to me, all you who are weary and burdened, and I will give you rest. Take my yoke upon you and learn from me, for I am gentle and humble in heart, and you will find rest for your souls. For my yoke is easy and my burden is light.

MATTHEW 11:28-30

"In your anger do not sin": Do not let the sun go down while you are still angry, and do not give the devil a foothold.

EPHESIANS 4:26-27

For if you forgive men when they sin against you, your heavenly Father will also forgive you. But if you do not forgive men their sins, your Father will not forgive your sins.

MATTHEW 6:14-15

Be kind and compassionate to one another, forgiving each other, just as in Christ God forgave you.   EPHESIANS 4:32

How to Handle Our Hurts

As we go through life, we get hurt. Indeed, most of us have been hurt so much that if we had a small bandage on our bodies for every time we've been hurt, we'd look like mummies! When we are hurt, we do our best to keep from falling apart or reacting in such a way that our behavior is socially unacceptable. Either way, we suppress our honest (truthful) reaction.

Suppressing these reactions, while it enables us to cope at the time, becomes counterproductive later. When we suppress our true reactions, it is like putting bandages on open, unhealed wounds without cleansing them first. Those wounds, then, though bandaged, become infected and fester under the bandages.

Ideally, we would have dealt honestly with each hurt at or soon after the time it happened. This is done by facing our true feelings, admitting them, and allowing Jesus to take charge. He has invited us to come to him with all of our heavy loads (Mt 11:28). We are further admonished by Paul to deal with our anger and, presumably, other such reactions before the end of every day (Eph 4:26). Above all, as both Jesus and Paul made plain, we are to forgive anyone who has hurt us (Mt 6:14-15; Eph 4:32).

The fact that we have ordinarily not kept such "short accounts" with our hurts, leaving them to fester within us, results in mild to severe disruption in three relationships: with God, with ourselves, and with others. Disruptions in these areas create most of the garbage the enemy takes advantage of. Bringing healing in those areas breaks the enemy's grip on us.

Bring your hurts and bitterness to Jesus.
He wants to lift from you burdens you
cannot bear and destructive emotions
that eat at you. He will heal your wounds
if only you will let him.

And when you stand praying, if you hold anything against anyone, forgive him, so that your Father in heaven may forgive you your sins. MARK 11:25

Therefore, as God's chosen people, holy and dearly loved, clothe yourselves with compassion, kindness, humility, gentleness and patience. Bear with each other and forgive whatever grievances you may have against one another. Forgive as the Lord forgave you. COLOSSIANS 3:12-13

I will refresh the weary and satisfy the faint. JEREMIAH 31:25

Take Out the Garbage

Demonic activity weakens when people give Jesus their heavy loads. Jesus says that "all ... who are tired from carrying heavy loads" are to come to him and receive the rest he promises (Mt 11:28) as we cast all our cares on him (1 Pt 5:7). It is especially important to give him the loads caused by our negative reactions to the hurts of life. We are to give him our anger, bitterness, and hateful feelings (Eph 4:17-32) and forgive others as we have been forgiven (Mt 6:14-15).

If we take care of the inner "garbage," the enemy's ability to influence us either from outside or inside is considerably lessened. I believe the absence of "inner garbage" was what Jesus was referring to when he said, "The ruler of this world is coming, and *he has nothing in Me*" (Jn 14:30, NKJV). Many people can get rid of such garbage by themselves through prayer. Others need the assistance of a Christian skilled in inner healing.

*Jesus does not want you to carry
heavy loads. He asks you to cast all
your cares and hurts upon him;
he cares so much for you.*

We are hard pressed on every side, but not crushed; perplexed, but not in despair; persecuted, but not abandoned; struck down, but not destroyed. We always carry around in our body the death of Jesus, so that the life of Jesus may also be revealed in our body. 2 CORINTHIANS 4:8-10

For our light and momentary troubles are achieving for us an eternal glory that far outweighs them all.

2 CORINTHIANS 4:17

So then, those who suffer according to God's will should commit themselves to their faithful Creator and continue to do good. 1 PETER 4:19

How to Stand Steady in Times of Trouble

Paul knew the misunderstanding of men, the harassment of political and religious leaders, and the spiritual oppression of demonic powers. He begins and ends 2 Corinthians 4 with an affirmation, "We do not lose heart." To identify with the Lord Jesus is to enter into his suffering.

Though the apostle does not specifically mention demons, the reality of spiritual warfare is made obvious by his words. He refers often to the pain of misunderstanding and rejection from both believers and nonbelievers. Certainly he must also have thought of the many circumstances when evil men wanted him killed. The devil used whomever or whatever he could to dissuade Paul from his commission. Paul's example teaches me that pain is at one and the same time both *purposeful* and deeply paradoxical. I am comforted to know that my troubles are producing an eternal glory that will one day supersede the worst misery endured on earth. But on an immediate, emotional level, hardship can produce a weight that crushes my confidence. It is easy to wonder why the Israelites were so rebellious when they had the Red Sea experience, the pillar of fire at night, and the cloud of God's presence by day. Yet we are made of the same stuff and fall prey to the same sins.

We have a profoundly important decision to make in the midst of trial: we can break *down* and give in to doubts about God's promise or purpose in pain, or we can hold steady and break *through* to a deeper level of character. Sooner or later most Christians go through a time of testing when they are tempted to shout to the heavens, "Where is the victory here?" Certainly this is evident in the Bible, which portrays many of God's people groping to understand why the righteous have such trouble. Each one had to wrestle with the issue and to decide that God was to be trusted. A Christian's capacity to overcome the world, the flesh, and the devil must be tested, and sometimes to the limit.

True spiritual victory emerges from the
crucible of suffering.

61

"My son, do not make light of the Lord's discipline, and do not lose heart when he rebukes you, because the Lord disciplines those he loves, and he punishes everyone he accepts as a son." Our fathers disciplined us for a little while as they thought best; but God disciplines us for our good, that we may share his holiness. No discipline seems pleasant at the time, but painful. Later on, however, it produces a harvest of righteousness and peace for those who have been trained by it.

HEBREWS 12:5-6, 10-11

How to Deal With Trials

Ask the Lord if your suffering is purposeful. When Paul sought the Lord for the removal of his thorn (2 Cor 12:14-17), God gave him peace and grace to accept the thorn as something productive of humility. If God gives you a similar answer, ask him, in light of Hebrews 12, "What am I to learn here? How can I grow, not in spite of, but in light of, this trial?" If, on the other hand, you are enduring unnecessary enemy harassment, you have the authority to rebuke it through direct command. Seek the counsel and discernment of others close to you, who may be able to see God's purposes more clearly.

Make a choice to turn your self-pity into triumph. If somehow you can choose to thank God for the trial and praise him for his purposes, he will pour out grace to grow. You may need to get quite practical here and decide to take specific steps to restore a strained relationship or seek out counseling for a longstanding emotional weakness that *can* and *should* be healed.

Anchor your soul in God's unfailing attributes. Review the Scriptures that reveal the character of the Lord, and affirm his goodness, through prayer and praise, his unfailing love, and his quickness to forgive and restore a floundering child.

Rebuke the father of lies. Let the devil and his minions know that you are choosing to trust the goodness of God, no matter what.

A mark of maturity is to rejoice in tribulation. Spiritual warfare is a great opportunity to exemplify the character of our Lord. When I walk in grace, the Father says, "Look, there, that's my child!" The devil is defeated in the face of a child who takes the Father at his word and walks by faith, no matter how tough the trials get. To exercise obedient submission to Jesus is to destroy the will and works of Satan and to demonstrate the goodness and glory of God.

Consider it pure joy, my brothers, whenever
you face trials of many kinds, because you
know that the testing of your faith develops
perseverance. Perseverance must finish its
work so that you may be mature and
complete, not lacking anything.
James 1:2-4

Yet you are holy, enthroned on the praises of Israel.

PSALM 22:3, NRSV

Some men came and told Jehoshaphat, "A vast army is coming against you." Alarmed, Jehoshaphat resolved to inquire of the Lord. Then Jehoshaphat stood up ... and said, "O Lord, God of our fathers, are you not the God who is in heaven? You rule over all the kingdoms of the nations. Power and might are in your hand, and no one can withstand you.... We have no power to face this vast army. We do not know what to do, but our eyes are upon you." "This is what the Lord says to you: 'Do not be afraid or discouraged because of this vast army. For the battle is not yours, but God's. Tomorrow march down against them.... Stand firm and see the deliverance the Lord will give you.'" Early in the morning they left. Jehoshaphat appointed men to sing to the Lord and to praise him for the splendor of his holiness as they went out at the head of the army, saying: "Give thanks to the Lord, for his love endures forever." As they began to sing and praise, the Lord set ambushes against the [invaders] and they were defeated. When the men of Judah came ... they saw only dead bodies lying on the ground.

2 CHRONICLES 20:2-3, 5-6, 12, 15-17, 20-22, 24

Praise: The Lifestyle of the Spiritual Warrior

Praise is an act of faith that affirms the character and redemptive power of God in all circumstances. If God truly dwells in the praises of his people, the regular practice of praise must be built into the lifestyle of the spiritual warrior. I used to feel weighed down by the burden of spiritual battles, but then I learned a secret. God waits for us to praise him so he can pour out his strength in us. Praise releases divine power to transform our perspective and our response to problems.

*The battle is not yours but God's.
Do not be afraid. Stand firm and praise
him. He will deliver you.*

For those God foreknew he also predestined to be conformed to the likeness of his Son, that he might be the firstborn among many brothers.   ROMANS 8:29

From the beginning God chose you to be saved through the sanctifying work of the Spirit and through belief in the truth.
2 THESSALONIANS 2:13

The one who is in you is greater than the one who is in the world.   1 JOHN 4:4

We Are a Work in Progress

As we all know, believers still have a lot of work to do to achieve the goal of becoming "conformed to the image of [Jesus]" (Rom 8:29, NKJV). They must still contend with their old sin nature. For reasons we do not understand, our sin nature is not eradicated when we accept Christ. We must fight for every inch of sanctification. But with the Holy Spirit within us to help us, we can make great progress.

When people give their lives to Jesus and become Christians, a miracle takes place. Jesus Christ himself comes to live inside them. A transfer of power and ownership is made. Those who once belonged to the "ruler of this world" (Jn 14:30) now belong to Jesus, and he rules in their lives. All has become new (2 Cor 5:17) in the deepest part of their beings—their spirits. The central and most important part of each person, the part that died when Adam sinned (Gn 2:17), is now made alive and becomes the home of Jesus.

Jesus, the new ruler, rescues them from the kingdom of the enemy and places them in the kingdom of God. Our Lord won the right to do this by defeating Satan at the resurrection. From the moment people decide to give their lives to Jesus, the one who lives within them is greater than the former ruler, the one who is in the world (1 Jn 4:4).

God has rescued you from the dominion
of darkness and brought you into his
kingdom where you have redemption,
forgiveness, and new life.
(See Colossians 1:13.)

For you know that it was not with perishable things such as silver or gold that you were redeemed ... but with the precious blood of Christ, a lamb without blemish or defect.

1 PETER 1:18-19

He did not enter by means of the blood of goats and calves; but he entered the Most Holy Place once for all by his own blood, having obtained eternal redemption.

HEBREWS 9:12

Finding Freedom From Familiar Spirits

While we should not become carried away with the idea of demons wreaking havoc in our lives, it is wise to be aware that they exist and that we may need to do battle with some of them. The following list may help you recognize some of the more common spirits that seem to take advantage of people.

1. Fear or mistrust.
2. Anger or malice.
3. Murder or destruction.
4. Death, morbidity, or suicide.
5. Division or strife.
6. Infirmity or sickness.
7. Control, aggression, or passivity.
8. Lust or pornography.
9. Greed or power.

10. Idolatry or rebellion.
11. Perversion or the macabre.
12. Religiosity or false worship.
13. Blame or criticism.
14. Entrapment or seduction.
15. Silence or mutism.
16. Jealousy or entitlement.
17. Mockery or sarcasm.
18. Confusion or double-mindedness.
19. Pride or perfectionism.
20. Self-control or self-denial.
21. Unforgiveness or bitterness.
22. Grief, sorrow, or depression.

Ask God to show you whether any of these spirits or others are at work in your life. Use a three-step process in order to battle whatever spirits God shows you are at work in your life. *Define* the lie's content and identify the spirit responsible for maintaining the lie. *Separate* yourself from the spirit's influence by repenting of your complicity and binding its power in Jesus' name. *Refute* the lie with statements of truth from the Scriptures (Eph 4:25).

*Command Satan to leave your presence,
along with all of his demons, in the name
of your Lord Jesus Christ. Claim the
power of the blood of Jesus which he shed
for you. Bring that blood between you
and all the forces of darkness.*

For though we live in the world, we do not wage war as the world does. The weapons we fight with are not the weapons of the world. On the contrary, they have divine power to demolish strongholds. We demolish arguments and every pretension that sets itself up against the knowledge of God, and we take captive every thought to make it obedient to Christ.

2 CORINTHIANS 10:3-5

But when he, the Spirit of truth, comes, he will guide you into all truth.
JOHN 16:13

"For my thoughts are not your thoughts, neither are your ways my ways," declares the Lord. "As the heavens are higher than the earth, so are my ways higher than your ways and my thoughts than your thoughts."
ISAIAH 55:8-9

For the foolishness of God is wiser than man's wisdom, and the weakness of God is stronger than man's strength.
1 CORINTHIANS 1:25

What Is a Stronghold?

My definition of a stronghold is "any area of our lives we cannot control that is destructive." According to 2 Corinthians 10:3-5, *all our strongholds can be demolished.* Healing can take place. Truth can replace faulty thinking.

You may think you've tried everything humanly possible. Perhaps you have, and that's the root of the problem. If the solutions you've tried have been "human" (fleshly), they have been ineffective. The destruction of strongholds requires more than your own strength and wisdom; it requires God's power. You will have to depend on the Holy Spirit first to reveal the strongholds in your life and then to provide the power to demolish them.

*Freedom from strongholds is not
just a hopeful thought but a reality
through the revelation of the Spirit
and the power of God.*

Flee the evil desires of youth, and pursue righteousness, faith, love and peace, along with those who call on the Lord out of a pure heart. 2 TIMOTHY 2:22

Therefore do not let sin reign in your mortal body so that you obey its evil desires. Do not offer the parts of your body to sin, as instruments of wickedness, but rather offer yourselves to God, as those who have been brought from death to life; and offer the parts of your body to him as instruments of righteousness. ROMANS 6:12-13

My guilt has overwhelmed me like a burden too heavy to bear. My wounds fester and are loathsome because of my sinful folly.... There is no health in my body. PSALM 38:4-5, 7

We have not received the spirit of the world but the Spirit who is from God, that we may understand what God has freely given us.... We have the mind of Christ. 1 CORINTHIANS 2:12, 16

Demons Attack Our Sexuality

Sex is a God-given part of our autonomic nervous system. Normal sexual functioning is a regular, rhythmic part of life. But when Jesus said, "Everyone who looks at a woman lustfully has already committed adultery with her in his heart" (Mt 5:28), he was describing something beyond the boundary of God's design for sex. The word for lust is *epithumos.* The prefix *epi* means "to add to," signifying that something is being added to a normal drive. Jesus challenged us not to add on to the God-given sexual drive by polluting our minds with lustful thoughts. The only way to control your sexual life is to control your thought life.

Sexual lust demands physical expression, and that's where Romans 6 comes into play. We are not to let sin reign in our mortal bodies (verse 12) by using our bodies as instruments of unrighteousness (verse 13). Whenever you use your body wrongly through a sexual offense you give Satan a foothold, and your sexual problem becomes a spiritual problem. A missionary shared with me at the end of a conference that he was finally free after twenty years of bondage to lust. He sought counseling for his problem during his preparation for missionary service and on every furlough, but he never gained lasting victory until he realized that it was a spiritual problem which needed a spiritual solution.

> First Corinthians 10:13 is the shining good news in the midst of our struggle with temptation: "No temptation has seized you except what is common to man. And God is faithful; he will not let you be tempted beyond what you can bear. But when you are tempted, he will also provide a way out so that you can stand up under it."

We have renounced secret and shameful ways; we do not use deception, nor do we distort the word of God. On the contrary, by setting forth the truth plainly we commend ourselves to every man's conscience in the sight of God.

2 CORINTHIANS 4:2

It is for freedom that Christ has set us free. Stand firm, then, and do not let yourselves be burdened again by a yoke of slavery. GALATIANS 5:1

The fruit of the Spirit is ... self-control.

GALATIANS 5:22-23

From Bondage

Breaking the Bondage of Pornography

Consider a man who was exposed to pornography in pre-adolescence, raised by a father bound by lust. The power of impurity burned into this man's sensual circuits will simply not respond to good reason or strong will. A bondage or stronghold exists in this area, originating in human reality and exploitable by evil spirits.

I recall a pastor who came to me, desperate to be free of his cycle of defeat over lust. He had read all the books, prayed harder, believed stronger, and even shared the burden with his wife. Yet he still felt enticed to peruse magazines looking for lewd photographs. His visit to my office proved to be the turning point, an "altar of remembrance."

After he had renounced his sin with sincere resolve, I prayed with authority: *Lord Jesus, in the power of your name, release your purity into my brother's mind. Holy Spirit, break the bondage of lust, and close the door on the enemy's influence.* Something happened. This man didn't become a monk. He wasn't freed from all temptation. But a fresh power of self-control was released into his life.

Jesus wants to release you from the things to which you feel enslaved, to purify you and empower you to walk forward in freedom.

Finally, brothers, whatever is true, whatever is noble, whatever is right, whatever is pure, whatever is lovely, whatever is admirable—if anything is excellent or praiseworthy—think about such things.　　　　PHILIPPIANS 4:8

Take up the shield of faith, with which you can extinguish all the flaming arrows of the evil one.　　　EPHESIANS 6:16

No temptation has seized you except what is common to man. And God is faithful; he will not let you be tempted beyond what you can bear. But when you are tempted, he will also provide a way out so that you can stand up under it.
1 CORINTHIANS 10:13

Stop Wrong Thoughts at the Door

Paul instructs us to take every thought captive to the obedience of Christ (2 Cor 10:5). The first step for escaping temptation is to apprehend every thought as soon as it steps through the doorway of your mind.

Once you have halted a penetrating thought, the next step is to evaluate it on the basis of Paul's eightfold criterion for what we should think about: "Whatever is true, whatever is noble, whatever is right, whatever is pure, whatever is lovely, whatever is admirable—if anything is excellent or praiseworthy—think about such things" (Phil 4:8). Ask yourself, "Does this thought line up with God's truth? Is it suggesting that I do something honorable? Right? Pure? If this thought becomes action, will the outcome be lovely and contribute to excellence in my life? Will other believers approve of my actions? Is it something for which I can praise God?" If the answer to any of these questions is no, dismiss that thought immediately. Don't have anything more to do with it. If it keeps coming back, keep saying no. When you learn to respond to tempting thoughts by stopping them at the door of your mind, evaluating them on the basis of God's Word, and dismissing those which fail the test, you have found the way of escape that God's Word promises.

God promises to provide for you an escape
from every temptation, constructive truth to
supplant every destructive thought, and
strength to overcome every weakness.

"In your anger do not sin": Do not let the sun go down while you are still angry, and do not give the devil a foothold.
                                                    EPHESIANS 4:26-27

See to it that ... no bitter root grows up to cause trouble and defile many.   HEBREWS 12:15

Angry but Not Sinning

People who are physically or emotionally mistreated normally react by getting angry. When, however, we cling to the anger, causing permanent resentment, bitterness, and unforgiveness, a weakness is created that can give the enemy opportunity to enter us. Such attitudes create what I call emotional or spiritual "garbage" that demons can feed on.

Demons cannot enter and stay without a "legal" right. They gain this right when we do not get rid of normal, yet potentially harmful, reactions such as anger. The anger itself is not a sin. We read in Ephesians 4:26, *"If* you become angry..." [emphasis mine]. The implication is clearly that we will become angry. But when that happens, we are told to "not let your anger lead you into sin, and do not stay angry all day." The reason for this admonition, then, is given in the next verse, "Don't give the Devil a chance" (Eph 4:27, TEV). And a few verses later we are told further, "Get rid of all bitterness, passion, and anger.

No more shouting or insults, no more hateful feelings of any sort. Instead, be kind and tender-hearted to one another, and forgive one another, as God has forgiven you through Christ" (Eph 4:31-32, TEV). Jesus strongly emphasizes the need to forgive. Right after the Lord's Prayer, he tells us, "If you forgive others the wrongs they have done to you, your Father in heaven will also forgive you. But if you do not forgive others, then your Father will not forgive the wrongs you have done" (Mt 6:14-15, TEV).

> *Forgiveness deals a mortal blow to the*
> *harassment of the enemy.*

Promises for Release

If you forgive anyone, I also forgive him. And what I have forgiven—if there was anything to forgive—I have forgiven in the sight of Christ for your sake, in order that Satan might not outwit us. For we are not unaware of his schemes.

2 CORINTHIANS 2:10-11

In anger his master turned him over to the jailers to be tortured, until he should pay back all he owed. This is how my heavenly Father will treat each of you unless you forgive your brother from your heart. MATTHEW 18:34-35

Be merciful, just as your Father is merciful. LUKE 6:36

Do not repay evil for evil. Do not take revenge, my friends, but leave room for God's wrath, for it is written: "It is mine to avenge; I will repay," says the Lord.

ROMANS 12:17, 19

80

From Bondage

Bitterness Versus Forgiveness

Most of the ground Satan gains in the lives of Christians is because of unforgiveness. We are warned to forgive others so that Satan cannot take advantage of us (2 Cor 2:10, 11). God requires us to forgive others from our hearts or he will turn us over to the tormentors (Mt 18:34-35). Why is forgiveness so critical to our freedom? Because of the cross. God didn't give us what we *deserve;* he gave us what we *needed* according to his mercy. We are to be merciful just as our heavenly Father is merciful (Lk 6:36). We are to forgive as we have been forgiven (Eph 4:31-32).

Forgiveness is a choice. Since God requires us to forgive, it is something we can do. (He would never require us to do something we cannot do.) "Why should I let them off the hook?" we protest. You let them off *your* hook, but they are never off God's hook. He will deal with them fairly—something we cannot do.

If you don't let offenders off your hook, you are hooked to them and the past, and that just means continued pain for you. Stop the pain; let it go. You don't forgive people merely for their sakes; you do it for *your* sake so you can be free. Your need to forgive isn't an issue between you and the offender; it's between you and God.

You can forgive. God promises to
give you the power to do so. Trust
his justice, and forgive.

We know that we have come to know him if we obey his commands. If anyone obeys his word, God's love is truly made complete in him. 1 JOHN 2:3, 5

Do not be overcome by evil, but overcome evil with good. ROMANS 12:21

When Forgiveness Is Really Hard

During the Nazi occupation of Holland, a remarkable Dutch woman and her family were sent to a concentration camp for hiding Jews in their home. Corrie ten Boom soon came to hate the guard who mocked and sneered at their naked bodies as they were taken to the showers. His leering face seemed forever seared into her memory. Her sister died in the camp, but Corrie survived and vowed never to return to Germany.

When she did return for a speaking engagement many years later, her first talk was on forgiveness. To her horror, the same guard was sitting in the audience. He could never have recognized Corrie as one of his emaciated, sick, and shorn prisoners. His radiant expression even suggested he had since been converted. After the talk, the smiling man extended his hand and said, "Ah, dear sister Corrie, isn't it wonderful how God forgives?"

Feeling only intense hatred for this man who had so wronged her and her family, Corrie ten Boom heard the

82

From Bondage

Lord tell her to put out her hand. "It took all of the years that I had quietly obeyed God in obscurity to do the hardest thing I have ever done in my life. I put out my hand. It was only after my simple act of obedience that I felt something almost like warm oil being poured over me. And with it came the unmistakable message: 'Well done, Corrie. That's how my children behave.' And the hate in my heart was absorbed and gone."

If the bitterness lingers, continue to repent of it daily, and release to God's justice anyone who has offended you. Unforgiveness, it seems, is the strongest of the strongholds. It is often a core issue for the Christian who is stagnant or struggling.

"It's too hard," you may say.
God responds, "With me
all things are possible."

Put to death, therefore, whatever belongs to your earthly nature: sexual immorality, impurity, lust, evil desires and greed, which is idolatry. Because of these, the wrath of God is coming. You used to walk in these ways, in the life you once lived. But now you must rid yourselves of all such things as these: anger, rage, malice, slander, and filthy language from your lips. Do not lie to each other, since you have taken off your old self with its practices and have put on the new self, which is being renewed in knowledge in the image of its Creator.   COLOSSIANS 3:5-10

Sin Is an Invitation to Demons

Wallowing in unconfessed sin is another common unconscious invitation to demons. So is repeatedly giving in to potentially addictive behavior. This undermines spiritual defenses, providing what one Christian teacher has pictured in a lecture as "a runway with lights showing the way for demons to enter." The more one wallows in such dangerous attitudes and behavior, the greater the risk of unconscious demonic infestation. Demons study human beings and are quick to take advantage of any opportunity to get inside.

To avoid such danger, we need to deal both with obvious sins and with any suspicious attitudes and behavior. We are responsible to God to work with him on the "garbage" in us, the works of our human nature.

84

From Bondage

The enemy actively encourages all such behavior and frequently finds entrance through the weaknesses they cause. Scripture is clear that whether or not there is demonization, these sins must be dealt with by repentance and self-discipline.

Demons cannot enter simply because a person commits a sin. They can, however, enter if a person chooses *not* to repent or to resolve any given sin and consequently wallows in it. Continuance in sinful attitudes creates opportunity for demonization. Sins of the flesh need to be repented of and resolved before they become demonic "runways."

The good news is that we can work in the power of the Holy Spirit, both to deal with any sin or attitude or behavior, and to banish any demons that may be attached to them.

Let your repentance come quickly, humbly, and with joy, for it will cover you with the protective shield of forgiveness and right standing with God.

Therefore confess your sins to each other and pray for each other so that you may be healed. The prayer of a righteous man is powerful and effective. JAMES 5:16

If we confess our sins, he is faithful and just and will forgive us our sins and purify us from all unrighteousness.

1 JOHN 1:9

Then I acknowledged my sin to you and did not cover up my iniquity. I said, "I will confess my transgressions to the Lord"—and you forgave the guilt of my sin. PSALM 32:5

From Bondage

A Strong Confession

People who have been caught in the trap of sin-confess, sin-confess may need to follow the instructions of James 5:16: "Confess your sins to each other and pray for each other so that you may be healed. The prayer of a righteous man is powerful and effective." Seek out a righteous person who will hold you up in prayer and to whom you can be accountable. Others may only need the assurance of 1 John 1:9: "If we confess our sins, he is faithful and just and will forgive us our sins and purify us from all unrighteousness." Confession is not saying "I'm sorry" but saying "I did it."

Lord, I renounce my acts of unrighteousness and by so doing ask You to break all bondages that Satan has brought into my life through my unrighteous behavior. I now present my body to You as a living sacrifice, holy and acceptable to You.

The Lord has totally cleansed and forgiven you. He loves you and accepts you unconditionally.

Let us not give up meeting together, as some are in the habit of doing, but let us encourage one another—and all the more as you see the Day approaching. HEBREWS 10:25

I have hidden your word in my heart that I might not sin against you. PSALM 119:11

Let us hold unswervingly to the hope we profess, for he who promised is faithful. HEBREWS 10:23

Pray continually. 1 THESSALONIANS 5:17

Maintain Your Freedom

To maintain your freedom, I suggest the following:

- Seek legitimate Christian fellowship where you can walk in the light and speak the truth in love.

- Study your Bible daily. Memorize key verses.

- Take every thought captive to the obedience of Christ. Assume responsibility for your thought life, reject the lie, choose the truth, and stand firm in your position in Christ.

- Don't drift away! It is very easy to get lazy in your thoughts and revert to old patterns of thinking. Share your struggles openly with a trusted friend. You need at least one friend who will stand with you.

- Don't expect another person to fight your battle for you. Others can help, but they can't think, pray, read the Bible, or choose the truth for you.

- Commit yourself to daily prayer. Pray often and with confidence.

> *The Lord gives you victory over sin, but he also calls you to participate in maintaining this victory. In daily choosing his way, you are exercising your spiritual muscle and yielding to the process of sanctification.*

Finally, be strong in the Lord and in his mighty power. Put on the full armor of God so that you can take your stand against the devil's schemes. EPHESIANS 6:10-11

For all of you who were baptized into Christ have clothed yourselves with Christ. GALATIANS 3:27

Through Spiritual Armor

Christ Defends You: Wearing His Armor

The classic chapter on protection is Ephesians 6. Paul uses the armor that the Roman legionaries wore to illustrate the means of protection God has provided for the Christian. It is very important at the outset to grasp the fact that this is not *our* armor but *God's*, given to us to protect us. It is not *our* righteousness or *our* faith or *our* gospel which can stand in the evil day. It is God's provision alone which will give us adequate protection. If we see this simple but profound fact it could well make all the difference between victory and defeat. And in a sense all the pieces of armor, when combined, are Christ himself. Elsewhere Paul does urge his readers to "put on Christ" (Gal 3:27). He is our protector.

Clothed in Christ, you are completely protected from evil.

*For the accuser of our brothers, who accuses them before our
God day and night, has been hurled down.*

REVELATION 12:10

*Stand firm then, with the belt of truth buckled around your
waist.* EPHESIANS 6:14

*Therefore, there is now no condemnation for those who are in
Christ Jesus.* ROMANS 8:1

Combating Lies: The Girdle of Truth

Satan has been a liar from the beginning and is the father
of lies, Jesus tells us (Jn 8:44). The first attack he made
on man took the form of a lie—"You shall not die," Satan
said, in defiance of the fact that God had clearly said they
would if they took the forbidden fruit. Satan is always causing us to doubt. "God can't be a God of love"; "God can't
really be in control of the universe"; "I'm too sinful to be
a child of God"; "My old nature can't possibly be dead";
"God can't save me from this predicament I'm in"; "I
can't do it"; and so on. And Satan has always twisted and
perverted the Word of God.

One of Satan's favorite forms of attack on Christians is
false accusation. He is called in Revelation "the accuser of
the brethren," and he accuses us continuously before God
(Rv 12:10). He will never get God to believe these lies

about us, but it is surprising how many of God's children are taken in. One of the most common complaints among Christians is self-despair, and far too often it comes from believing what Satan says about us rather than what God says. The armor to meet this attack is "the girdle of truth."

Equally powerful these days seems to be the maligning of God's character by Satan. How many Christians one meets who do not believe God really loves them! As Satan continuously works against us, so we must put on "the girdle of God's truth."

God is what he says he is.
You are what God says you are.
God does what he says he will do.
You can do what God says you can do.

Stand firm then ... with the breastplate of righteousness in place.   EPHESIANS 6:14

God made him who had no sin to be sin for us, so that in him we might become the righteousness of God.

2 CORINTHIANS 5:21

It is because of him that you are in Christ Jesus, who has become for us wisdom from God—that is, our righteousness, holiness and redemption.   1 CORINTHIANS 1:30

The one who was born of God keeps him safe, and the evil one cannot harm him.   1 JOHN 5:18

Avoiding Temptation: The Breastplate of Righteousness

If Satan cannot pierce our armor by lies, he will try evil. He will bombard our minds with evil thoughts; he will try to influence our motives and sway our wills. The answer to this is God's righteousness, not our own! How many have tried to ward off these blows with the flimsy armor of their own goodness. Satan's arrows pierce it immediately. But, if we are Christians, we have God's righteousness with which to defend ourselves. Then let us wear it like a piece of armor. Evil thoughts are not sin until they are entertained. They are like the gate-crashers at a party; we can accept them and let them stay, or firmly show them where the door is. This is what we must do when Satan attacks us with evil—show him the door.

Satan cannot pierce the armor of God's righteousness. He may bruise us, but he cannot wound us.

But Peter and John replied, "Judge for yourselves whether it is right in God's sight to obey you rather than God. For we cannot help speaking about what we have seen and heard.... Now, Lord, ... enable your servants to speak your word with great boldness."   ACTS 4:19-20, 29

Always be prepared to give an answer to everyone who asks you to give the reason for the hope that you have.
                                        1 PETER 3:15

I give you this charge: Preach the Word; be prepared in season and out of season.   2 TIMOTHY 4:1-2

Sharing the Truth: The Gospel of Peace

If Satan cannot disturb us, then he will try to make us as comfortable and cozy as possible—so that we won't disturb him! He will stop his attacks and sue for peace, but on completely unacceptable terms for a Christian. "Leave me alone," he will say, "and I will leave you alone." We dare not parley with Satan. The early Christians would not have been persecuted had they stopped their evangelism. But they suffered at the hands of the Jewish authorities because they refused to do so.

Through Spiritual Armor

It is all too easy to fall for this subtle attack of the enemy and go along with "carpet slipper Christianity." Some today are "at ease in Zion," journeying to heaven in first-class comfort. Satan has seen to it that such Christians have laid down their arms and are no longer concerned to attack and invade enemy-held territory.

The answer to this form of temptation is to get our shoes on, leave the comforts of home, and go out after those who are Satan's captives. Ronald Knox translates Ephesians 6:15, "in readiness to publish the gospel." And it is the gospel of peace—for the only real peace that can be found in this world is through surrender to Christ, who is the Prince of Peace.

*In every encounter with others, be eager
to bring peace—the peace of forgiveness,
compassion, and the knowledge of Christ.
Remember: Blessed are the peacemakers.*

Peace I leave with you; my peace I give you.   JOHN 14:27

God was reconciling the world to himself in Christ, not counting men's sins against them. And he has committed to us the message of reconciliation.   2 CORINTHIANS 5:19

Let us therefore make every effort to do what leads to peace and to mutual edification.   ROMANS 14:19

Be a Peacemaker

Jesus declared, "Blessed are the peace*makers*, for they will be called sons of God" (Mt 5:9). Now why would peacemaking qualify us as sons of God? Because God is in the business of making peace. Reconciliation is the theological word for it. "Peace on earth," the angels sang when Christ was born. Paul summed it up: "God was reconciling the world to himself in Christ, not counting men's sins against them. And he has committed to us the message of reconciliation" (2 Cor 5:19).

Sometimes I think this is the area of the devil's greatest success: peace-*breaking*. Peace is elusive. Peace doesn't just happen. God made peace when he sent his Son into the world on a mission of forgiveness and reconciliation. But the world remains full of strife: in the mean streets of dark cities; between nations; between races and ethnic groups.

It happens in families all the time. Hostility prevails and marriages end, spinning the children into a chasm of confusion, resentment, and shame. And the curse goes on as divorce grips one generation after another. "See to it," the Bible says, "that no bitter root grows up to cause trouble and defile many" (Heb 12:15).

Because our struggle is *not* with flesh and blood but with the underlying divisiveness of dark angels, we should be putting on the shoes of the readiness of peace. Wherever the path of life takes us, we should be ready to make peace, not war. Peace happens because someone makes it happen. If our hearts are filled with God, we will be a ready antidote for the poison of misunderstanding. We will be standing in readiness, the readiness of peace. And we'll thoroughly frustrate the dark angels with the potency of peacemaking.

Peace brings rest. Peace gives hope.
Peace allows love to reign.

Dear friends, do not be surprised at the painful trial you are suffering, as though something strange were happening to you.   1 PETER 4:12

Consider it pure joy, my brothers, whenever you face trials of many kinds, because you know that the testing of your faith develops perseverance. Perseverance must finish its work so that you may be mature and complete, not lacking anything.
                                                        JAMES 1:2-4

Persevering Under Fire: The Shield of Faith

It's easy to spot the devil's scheme here. The opposite of faith is doubt and, in its more deliberate form, unbelief. Everybody has doubts. Doubts about ourselves. Doubts about the future. Doubts about God. But when doubt becomes unbelief, life-sustaining faith evaporates. Unbelief is the vacuum of debilitating uncertainty. The skeptic becomes an atheist.

The time when our faith is tested the most, of course, is when everything is going wrong. Trouble moves us deeply. It stirs up our deepest feelings and exposes our greatest weaknesses. Unfortunately, when we are in trouble we are the most vulnerable emotionally and spiritually. We need to hold still, to stay steady at all costs. I like the way J.B. Phillips translates Ephesians 6:13: "Therefore you must wear the whole armor of God that you may be able to resist evil in its day of power, and that even when you have fought to a standstill, you may still stand your ground. Take your stand then...." When everything's at a standstill, stand still!

The greatest test of our faith is under the rain of fire, "the flaming arrows of the wicked one." When the dark angels turn up the heat, everything in us screams, "Turn and run." But Peter reassures us, "Dear friends, do not be surprised at the painful trial you are suffering, as though something strange were happening" (1 Pt 4:12). Why? James explains, "Because you know that the testing of your faith develops perseverance. Perseverance must finish its work so that you may be mature and complete, not lacking anything" (Jas 1:3-4).

I am inclined to believe, therefore, that "the shield of faith" refers more to long-term "faithfulness" than to outbursts of the gift of faith to receive immediate and extraordinary answers to prayer. The shield of faith is faith that endures, faith that fights its way through the feelings of discouragement and failure. Tenacity. Perseverance. The shield of faithfulness.

Speak truth to yourself in times of trouble. Meditate on God's love, his wisdom, and his sovereign care. Hold on to his good character like a life preserver in raging waters. The Lord will preserve you, and soon you will see the fruit of this test of faith.

The god of this age has blinded the minds of unbelievers, so that they cannot see the light of the gospel of the glory of Christ. 2 CORINTHIANS 4:4

But I am afraid that just as Eve was deceived by the serpent's cunning, your minds may somehow be led astray from your sincere and pure devotion to Christ. 2 CORINTHIANS 11:3

Guarding Your Thoughts: The Helmet of Salvation

How can you guard your thoughts? How do you go about putting on the helmet of salvation? I have several suggestions:

First, as Paul writes in 2 Corinthians 10, *you need to take every thought captive to the law of Christ*—put everything you think under his lordship. This is why we can't live "by bread alone, but … by every word that comes from the mouth of God" (Mt 4:4).

As David observes, blessed is the person who meditates day and night on the Word of the Lord (see Psalm 1). The Word of God keeps our thinking moving in the right direction and protects us from the kind of thinking that is harmful to ourselves and others.

Second, as much as it's possible, *you need to think about good things:* "Whatever is true, whatever is noble, whatever is admirable—if anything is excellent or praiseworthy—

think about these things" (Phil 4:8, italics mine). "Above all else," Solomon wrote in the Old Testament, "guard your heart, for it is the well-spring of life" (Prv 4:23).

Third, *be careful what you take in with your eyes and ears.* Guard your mind. "Let us throw off everything that hinders and the sin that so easily entangles.... Let us fix our eyes on Jesus" (Heb 12:1-2).

Fourth, *don't trust all your thoughts.* Jeremiah wrote, "The heart is deceitful above all things and beyond cure. Who can understand it?" (Jer 17:9). If you just listen to yourself and have a hard time listening to others, you are setting yourself up for spiritual delusion. An open mind to the counsel and advice of others is a closed door to the mental seduction of dark angels.

> *At all times keep straight in your mind who you are. You are a child of God. Christ has saved you from sin and death. You are on the journey of being sanctified. You are destined for a glorious eternity with God. These truths will guard your mind.*

The word of God is living and active. Sharper than any double-edged sword, it penetrates even to dividing soul and spirit, joints and marrow; it judges the thoughts and attitudes of the heart.   HEBREWS 4:12

"Is not my word like fire," declares the Lord, "and like a hammer that breaks a rock in pieces?"   JEREMIAH 23:29

The Weapon of Truth: The Word of God

This weapon is the one offensive weapon referred to in the famous passage on spiritual warfare in Ephesians 6. The armor is for protection, but the sword of the Spirit "which is the word of God" is useful for both attack and defense. In Hebrews 4:12 the Word of God is again likened to a sword—it is "living and active. Sharper than any double-edged sword, it penetrates even to dividing soul and spirit, joints and marrow; it judges the thoughts and attitudes of the heart."

It has been said of preaching that it should "disturb the comfortable and comfort the disturbed." This aptly describes the ministry of the Word. When we are counseling and trying to help people who are oppressed by satanic power, we must know how to apply the Word of God not only in diagnosing the cause of the trouble, but also in prescribing the remedy. Jean Darnall has devised a very helpful method in this respect. She calls it "scriptural prescriptions," and like medicine they are to be taken by the patient "three times a day." We simply write out for the one we are trying to help (or for ourselves if we are treating ourselves!) a set of relevant Scriptures. It is then suggested that these be read aloud three times a day: morning, noon, and before going to bed. First, they are spoken to God, as witness that he has written this and so will fulfill it; second, to ourselves, as witnessing to the fact that it applies to us and we believe it; and, third, to the devil, as Jesus did in the wilderness, so that he has eventually to flee.

There is nothing quite like the Word of God, proclaimed in the power of the Holy Spirit, for forcing the enemy to reveal his influence and lose his foothold.

The name of the Lord is a strong tower; the righteous run to it and are safe.   PROVERBS 18:10

Holy Father, protect them by the power of your name—the name you gave me—so that they may be one as we are one. While I was with them, I protected them and kept them safe by that name you gave me.   JOHN 17:11-12

Jesus: Name Above All Names

Christ's name is a real power in spiritual warfare. When we talk about the protection of the name of Jesus, we do not mean that there is something magical about the word and that it is protective in itself. No, the name of Jesus means the protective power of his presence and all that he is today because of all that he did on the cross.

The value of the name of Jesus is that it combines the efficacy of his death with his resurrection life. It means "Savior"—and refers to One who is alive forever and raised "far above all." It is the living Christ who protects his people—standing by them and working with them. But it is Christ who shed his blood and died on the cross. Without the shedding of blood there would have been no remission of sins or power over Satan. In this sense, the blood of Christ is an indispensable part of our salvation and, *therefore*, of our protection.

> *Make the name of Jesus your tower of refuge and strength. All he has done for you, is doing, and will do is cause for a deep sense of security and safety.*

The angel of the Lord encamps around those who fear him,
and he delivers them.   PSALM 34:7

Last night an angel of the God whose I am and whom I serve
stood beside me and said, "Do not be afraid, Paul. You must
stand trial before Caesar; and God has graciously given you
the lives of all who sail with you." So keep up your courage,
men, for I have faith in God that it will happen just as he
told me.   ACTS 27:23-25

Angels Come to Our Aid

In the general skepticism within the church today, in which the supernatural has been debunked, the presence and value of angels are seldom if ever recognized. Like the servant of the prophet Elisha, we need to have our eyes opened to the protective ring of angels which is at all times around God's people. As the psalmist says, "The angel of the Lord encamps around those who fear him, and he delivers them" (34:7).

In the Acts of the Apostles angels seem to be as much in evidence as their satanic counterparts, the evil spirits. They seemed to be specialists in jail-breaking, for twice they managed to get the apostles and Peter out of prison.

They also helped in directing God's plans in evangelism. It was an angel, for example, who directed Philip to the desert of Gaza to contact the Ethiopian eunuch. When Paul was in danger of losing his life in a storm at sea, it was an angel that reassured him. If the demonic powers have not given up the struggle and returned to hell since New Testament days, are we to imagine that the angels are less powerfully present than they were in the days of the apostles of our Lord?

The Lord dispatches angels to guard you. They surround you and help to accomplish God's will in you. Welcome them in faith and thank the Lord often for their protection. You may even become more aware of their work in your life.

"The Spirit of the Lord is on me, because he has anointed me to preach good news to the poor. He has sent me to proclaim freedom for the prisoners and recovery of sight for the blind, to release the oppressed, to proclaim the year of the Lord's favor."   Luke 4:18-19

When Jesus had called the Twelve together, he gave them power and authority to drive out all demons and to cure diseases.   Luke 9:1

Delivering Others

Deliverance is not among the Bible's list of gifts for believers. Rather, we are *all* to do it (Lk 9:1). But most of us don't know that bringing deliverance is the privilege and responsibility of every Christian. Few experience the joy of seeing people freed from the grip of demons. Do not fear the enemy. Be confident in the awesome power of God; be bold to launch out with God in freeing people from demons. Be motivated to do the works Jesus promised we would do (Jn 14:12), in the authority and power he has given us (Lk 9:1), and in the process, be drawn into a deeper, more intimate relationship with him. *You can be used to bring freedom to demonized people—Jesus said you could.*

God really loves people. He loves people so much that he is not satisfied until every bit of the rest Jesus promised

Set Others Free

in Matthew 11:28, the freedom Paul speaks about in Galatians 5:1, and the new creation Paul points to in 2 Corinthians 5:17 is being experienced by his people. And that's what deliverance is all about—bringing people into all of the freedom Jesus desires for his chosen ones.

There is no greater work than freeing others from the grip of Satan and leading them to freedom in Christ. God has called you to this work, given you his authority, and equipped you with his power. It's not your work but his work through you, and he will accomplish it.

The kind of fasting I want is this: Remove the chains of oppression and the yoke of injustice, and let the oppressed go free.... If you put an end to oppression, to every gesture of contempt, and to every evil word; if you give food to the hungry and satisfy those who are in need, then the darkness around you will turn to the brightness of noon.... You will be known as the people who rebuilt the walls, who restored the ruined houses. ISAIAH 58:6, 9b-10, 12b, TEV

Set Others Free

We Inherit the Power to Free and Heal

God desires that Christians work with him to minister to the captives and wounded. When the oppressed are freed, "territory" is taken from Satan, and both God and we who participate in the release share the joy of the freed. As promised in the text quoted above, the darkness around us turns to brightness and we become known as "people who rebuilt the walls, who restored the ruined houses." The call to minister in power—freeing the demonized and healing the wounded—is part of our inheritance as children of God. Not only are healing and joy brought to the ones suffering from attack, but also to those who minister with Jesus.

When you step out to do the work of Jesus, be prepared for great blessing. You will discover that ministering God's love and freedom builds your faith, enriches your relationship with God, and brings you joy.

Each one should use whatever gift he has received to serve others, faithfully administering God's grace in its various forms.

1 PETER 4:10

There are different kinds of gifts, but the same Spirit. There are different kinds of service, but the same Lord. There are different kinds of working, but the same God works all of them in all men.... All these are the work of one and the same Spirit, and he gives them to each one, just as he determines.

1 CORINTHIANS 12:4-6, 11

Obedience Precedes Gifting

But, you may be asking, what about gifting? First of all, there is no gift of delivering people from demons. Apparently every believer is empowered to do that without special gifting. Second, the list of gifts in 1 Corinthians 12 speaks of "gifts of healings" (verse 9). Evidently, as we obey Jesus' command, we will discover that each of us is gifted in different ways to bring healing to those to whom he has led us. This has certainly been my observation of the people I have seen move in obedience. Those who pray for healing find that God backs them up. But they also vary in effectiveness, with some having greater success with certain ailments than with others.

On the basis of Scripture, experience, and observation,

Set Others Free

I conclude that *obedience is to precede gifting*. We, like Jesus and his disciples, are to obey God by freeing people from the enemy. We will discover in that obedience, then, what our special gifting may be. As we obey, God provides my colleagues and me with the authority, power, and gifting necessary to release people from demons. Those who simply observe, without launching out in obedience, never discover the authority, power, and gifting God gives. These come only as a person moves out with God.

*You are specially gifted by God. He
desires that you be effective in ministry.
Step out in faith, practice, and watch
your gifts come to life.*

He who refreshes others will himself be refreshed.

PROVERBS 11:25

I pray also that the eyes of your heart may be enlightened in order that you may know ... his incomparably great power for us who believe.

EPHESIANS 1:18-19

The apostles said to the Lord, "Increase our faith!" ... "So you also, when you have done everything you were told to do, should say, 'We are unworthy servants; we have only done our duty.'"

LUKE 17:5, 10

A Sure Way to Increase Your Faith

A deliverance ministry will increase your faith in Jesus. All of us who have moved in this direction have experienced tremendous renewal in our own spiritual lives. *It is an incredible thing to be involved constantly in doing what we know we cannot do.* We cannot cast out demons by ourselves. If the Holy Spirit doesn't "show up" to do the job, we're sunk! So the very fact that demons are regularly cast out, never to return, constantly humbles, excites, and enriches us. It proves over and over again that God actually is present and doing his work through us.

When the Lord pours out his Holy Spirit on the wounded, he splashes blessings on everyone else, too. It's like getting too close to a waterfall! You get sprayed just being there! Through this ministry my life has been dramatically changed and God has become much bigger! I have felt personally for the first time an answer to Paul's prayer that his readers will experience the "incomparably great power" available to "us who believe" (Eph 1:19). As I've sought to walk in obedience in this ministry, the Lord has led me deeper and deeper into intimacy with Jesus and excitement over my relationship with him.

Do you need renewal? Do you long for more of Jesus? Do you want to see his power at work? If so, step out in faith and minister to others. He will renew you in his power and love and use you beyond your wildest imagination.

For God did not give us a spirit of timidity, but a spirit of power, of love and of self-discipline.   2 TIMOTHY 1:7

So do not fear, for I am with you; do not be dismayed, for I am your God. I will strengthen you and help you; I will uphold you with my righteous right hand.   ISAIAH 41:10

Have No Fear

M any of us desperately want to respond by "fight not flight," but we fear the battle. To make our problem worse, many of us are ashamed to be afraid. It should come as no surprise to us that both the fear and the shame come straight from the enemy, the father of lies! One of his chief strategies is to make Christians afraid of him and demonic attack. He likes Christians to be frightened by media images of his amazing power and evil.

Actually, demons are mostly bluff! The power and authority we have in Jesus is *infinitely* greater than the enemy's. We need to remember that Jesus completely defeated Satan on the cross. As we enter the battle in Jesus' name, then, we have no reason to fear.

Those who watch us minister continually are amazed to see how calmly we can work. They often say, in effect, "I can't believe it. I've always pictured deliverance as scary, with demons exhibiting great power and evil." Knowing how much power is available to us, we simply take control and forbid them to cause problems. Though they may be able to cause a bit of a ruckus, there is really no contest.

Satan is our defeated foe. Jesus Christ has won the victory over evil. You can enter into the battle without fear and intimidation because you are on the winning side.

119

For it is we ... who worship by the Spirit of God, who glory in Christ Jesus, and who put no confidence in the flesh.

PHILIPPIANS 3:3

And pray in the Spirit on all occasions with all kinds of prayers and requests. With this in mind, be alert and always keep on praying for all the saints.   EPHESIANS 6:18

How to Prepare for Ministry

There is a need for genuine love and a gentle spirit in helping others in this way. We can get rough with Satan, but not with those who have become his victims. There is no need for noise. Satan and his angels will not be frightened off by this. But they will go as soon as the word of authority is spoken in faith.

We should never go lightly into this ministry. First, we should seek personal cleansing, in the same way as a surgeon will wash before an operation. We should repent of any sin and relinquish any trust or confidence in ourselves. We must confess, if necessary, any unbelief in the power of our Lord and the authority of his Word.

We should then put on the armor of God, piece by piece, leaving nothing to chance. You can pray something like this:

Set Others Free

Heavenly Father,

I claim by faith now the protection of your armor, that I may stand against Satan and all his hosts, and in the name of Jesus overcome them.

I take your truth to counter the lies and errors of a cunning enemy.

I take your righteousness to overcome the evil thoughts and accusations of Satan.

I take the equipment of the gospel of peace and forsake the safety and comforts of life in order to wage war with the enemy.

Above all, I take your faith to bar the way to doubts and unbelief entering my soul.

I take your salvation and trust you to protect my body and soul from Satan's varied attacks.

I take your Word and pray that the Holy Spirit will enable me to use it effectively against the enemy and to sever every bondage and deliver every captive of Satan.

In the strong and all-conquering name of Jesus Christ, my Lord. Amen.

Paul refers to "praying in the Holy Spirit." At this point, and before praying for the person in need, it is advisable to pray in the Spirit, asking for guidance. It will strengthen us for the work that lies ahead. Paul also cautions, "Keep alert with all perseverance." This we must continue to do.

Careful and diligent preparation before ministry clears the way for God to work powerfully through us.

The things that come from the Spirit of God ... are spiritually discerned.   1 CORINTHIANS 2:14

Now to each one the manifestation of the Spirit is given for the common good,... to another the ability to distinguish between spirits.   1 CORINTHIANS 12:7, 10

Learn to Discern

Jesus, of course, had the gift of "discerning of spirits" and manifested it on many occasions. It is a gift of discrimination and indispensable in spiritual warfare. It helps us distinguish between various possible agencies and discover the true source and motivation of life and action. Jesus' ability is described as "He knew what was in man" (Jn 2:25). He was able to interpret human motives and assess the genuineness of people's words and actions. He seemed instinctively to recognize hypocrisy on the one hand and reality on the other. He knew when men had faith and when they did not; when they were telling the truth and when they were lying. The "Word made flesh" was able to discern "the thoughts and intents of the heart" as the written Word does, according to Hebrews 4:12.

Jesus gives us the same commission as he received from the Father, anoints us with the same power, and promises that we will do the same works. Thus, the Holy Spirit desires, through the operation of this gift, to enable

Set Others Free

Christians to distinguish accurately between what comes "from above" and what rises "from below." What comes from God, what comes from man, and what comes from Satan. In any given situation there may be a mixture, but the Holy Spirit will help us analyze the situation and label the parts correctly.

Pray for wisdom and discernment.
God promises to give you these gifts.

If your eyes are good, your whole body will be full of light. But if your eyes are bad, your whole body will be full of darkness.
MATTHEW 6:22-23

To the pure, all things are pure, but to those who are corrupted and do not believe, nothing is pure. In fact, both their minds and consciences are corrupted. They claim to know God, but by their actions they deny him. They are detestable, disobedient and unfit for doing anything good.
TITUS 1:15-16

Everyone who has this hope in him purifies himself, just as he is pure. 1 JOHN 3:3

The Power of a Pure Heart

Without purity of life, discernment will be unreliable. In detecting, opposing, and overcoming evil power, we need to be pure ourselves. If we are looking for a small piece of sawdust in someone else's eye, while our own has a beam of wood in it, then we shall not be able to help the other person. We must have the beam removed first, and then, Jesus says, "you will see clearly to take the speck out of your brother's eye" (Mt 7:3-5).

The one who is free to move unmolested into enemy territory is the one who has a passion for righteousness and a hatred of evil. But a person who hankers after illicit pleasures, does Christian work for his own advantage, is undisciplined in his daily life, or is constantly self-indulgent will seldom be used to deliver others. On the contrary he may well be a stumbling block to the other person's release and might well become a victim of the very thing from which he is trying to release the other person. Paul kept his body disciplined at all times, "lest after preaching to others I myself should be disqualified" (1 Cor 9:27).

This purity should extend to our motives and desires also. Our chief desire should always be the glory of God, not our own.

Purity comes with a great promise:
"Blessed are the pure in heart, for they
will see God" (Mt 5:8).

And He said to them, "This kind cannot come out by any-thing but prayer [and fasting]."   MARK 9:29, NASB

When an evil spirit comes out of a man, it goes through arid places seeking rest and does not find it. Then it says, "I will return to the house I left." When it arrives, it finds the house swept clean and put in order. Then it goes and takes seven other spirits more wicked than itself, and they go in and live there. And the final condition of that man is worse than the first.   LUKE 11:24-26

How to Cast Out a Demon

How do you cast out a demon? A few tips are hardly adequate to deal with such a complex and explosive subject, but there are some general guidelines I think everyone should understand. I suggest the following:

First, ask yourself if it is a condition of demonization you can handle. If not, make a referral to someone who is competent in spiritual ministry, or you may wish to ask one or two others to assist you. If you are not sure, ask God if he is leading you to become involved. If God doesn't make it clear to you that you should become involved, don't.

Second, prepare yourself. Pray, asking for the anointing of power and the discerning of spirits. Jesus taught his disciples that some evil spirits do not respond to just anyone, anytime. Some people are delivered from dark angels only after fervent prayer and fasting.

Third, ask the demonized person to prepare for ministry with prayer and fasting. This is not possible, of course, if the individual is heavily oppressed, or if they ask for prayer not knowing that their problems are deeply spiritual.

Fourth, minister deliverance privately whenever possible. If I'm caught off-guard in a public meeting by an unexpected demonic manifestation, I always try to have the demonized person escorted to another room. Demons seem to like attention. Furthermore, observing a deliverance can be very frightening to people who are not familiar with that kind of ministry.

Fifth, in the name of Jesus command the dark angel, by name if necessary, to leave. Remember that the power of God has to do with Christ in you and the Spirit working through you, not the volume of your voice or the intensity of the religious feeling you might have at the moment.

Sixth, invite the Holy Spirit to come and fill the void, so that the dark angel can't take up residence again so easily.

Deliverance is serious business,
so keep asking God for discernment
and power. He will show you how
to accomplish his work.

Or again, how can anyone enter a strong man's house and carry off his possessions unless he first ties up the strong man? Then he can rob his house.   MATTHEW 12:29

By his death he destroy[ed] him who holds the power of death—that is, the devil—and free[d] those who all their lives were held in slavery.   HEBREWS 2:14-15

How to Pray for Others

When we pray we are not trying to persuade God to join us in *our* service for him; prayer is the activity of joining God in *his* ministry. By faith we lay hold of property in Satan's clutches which rightfully belongs to God, and we hold on until Satan turns loose. He will hold on to these people until we demand their release on the basis of our authority in Christ. Once Satan is bound through prayer, he must let go.

In his book *Demon Possession and the Christian*, C. Fred Dickason gives several helpful suggestions for how to pray for someone who is being harassed by demons:

1. Pray that the demons may be cut off from all communication and help from other demons and Satan.

2. Pray that the demons would be confused and weakened in their hold on the person.

3. Pray that the person would be strengthened in his faith to understand his position in Christ and to trust and obey God's Word.

4. Pray that the person may be able to distinguish between his thoughts and feelings and those of Satan.

5. Pray that the person might recognize the demonic presence and not be confused, but willingly seek godly counsel and help.

6. Pray that God would protect and guide his child and set angelic forces at work to break up every scheme of the enemy.*

*Prayer is the life line between
God's power and you.*

* Dickason, *Demon Possession and the Christian*, p. 255

In the past God overlooked such ignorance, but now he commands all people everywhere to repent.   ACTS 17:30

God will grant them repentance leading them to a knowledge of the truth, and ... they will come to their senses and escape from the trap of the devil, who has taken them captive to do his will.   2 TIMOTHY 2:25-26

He is patient with you, not wanting anyone to perish, but everyone to come to repentance.   2 PETER 3:9

Repentance Is Key to Getting Free

However powerless we are in the face of satanic onslaughts, sin should always be recognized, confessed, and forsaken. Of course, one would like to say, "You couldn't help it," or, "It wasn't your fault." But there can be no full deliverance, where a person's sin is a major factor, unless there is a frank recognition of it and a willingness with the help of God's grace to give it up. This is not easy. When sin is indulged in repeatedly, there is a dulling of conscience and conviction. One is tempted to allow excuses. Lovingly but firmly, for the sake of the person concerned, there should be an insistence on this repentance.

The person may have been more sinned against than sinning. In that case the temptation will often be to store up resentment and bitterness. If this has been done, then it will need to be confessed also.

Every person we minister to should be made aware of God's love, the joy of forgiveness, reconciliation, and restoration. God understands us and is never shocked at our confession. He knows all about it. It is only the proud, the unreal, and the insincere that he refuses. We need to bind up the spiritual wounds of repentance and pour into them the full measure of God's free pardon through the cross of his Son and his unrelenting love. We will need to read together the Word of God, explaining as simply as we know how the meaning of the cross and the power of the blood to cleanse. We should persist until we are sure that forgiveness has really been accepted and the way of God has been believed.

Don't underestimate the power of humble confession. Repentance turns the key in the deadlock of bondage.

He calls his own sheep by name and leads them out. When he has brought out all his own, he goes on ahead of them, and his sheep follow him because they know his voice.

JOHN 10:3-4

And so we know and rely on the love God has for us. God is love. Whoever lives in love lives in God, and God in him.

1 JOHN 4:16

Ask God for Assignments

As you grow in the depth of your own personal prayer life, you will more and more clearly perceive God's burdens. Ask the Lord for assignments. You'll never be the same. Every day becomes an adventure. It's like walking through life with one ear open to human reality, while the other ear is wired to receive transmissions from the command post of heaven.

Let love always be your aim as you put divine authority into action. In commenting on the qualifications for doing strategic warfare, Francis Frangipane offers this critical word of advice: "Authority is muscle in the arm of love. The more one loves, the more authority is granted to him.... However, no man should ever engage in confrontational warfare who does not love what he has been called to protect. If you do not love your city, do not pray against the ruling forces of darkness."*

Set Others Free

Will you hear and heed this word? If you move out ahead of the Lord in your *own* power, expect counter-attack. I have seen people suffer from depression, tension in marital or family relationships, extreme confusion, and health problems. The satanic power "out there" will push back. If we move at God's command and remain accountable and accessible to others, he will surely shield us from the powers of darkness and bring success to our efforts.

If we have the courage to move on what we believe to be divine assignments, we step into divine anointing. If the initiative truly comes from God, we experience a divine strength that lifts us out of human weakness.

*Francis Frangipane, The House of the Lord (Lake Mary, Florida: Creation House, 1991), 122.

For he will command his angels concerning you to guard you in all your ways; they will lift you up in their hands, so that you will not strike your foot against a stone.

PSALM 91:11-12

See that you do not look down on one of these little ones. For I tell you that their angels in heaven always see the face of my Father in heaven. MATTHEW 18:10

Are not all angels ministering spirits sent to serve those who will inherit salvation? HEBREWS 1:14

Praying for Children

Children are particularly vulnerable to all kinds of experiences and pressures. There is no reason to think they are free from enemy attacks; in fact, in many ways they are more open and need very much the protection of the believing prayers of their parents.

Often praying for children while they are asleep is effective. This is possible with young children who are the innocent victims of the sins of others. In fact, audible prayer and reassuring words, especially the Word of God itself, can reach and bring blessing to people in sleep. Children, for example, who suffer from nightmares can experience healing of the memories through this kind of therapy, as long as, of course, it is ministered through the Holy Spirit.

In our ministry to children we have to be very careful not to bring fear to them. If we pray for them audibly when they are conscious, then we should explain simply what we are going to do and frame it in language which will not scare them, but rather comfort and reassure them. Taught properly, young children have a surprisingly mature grasp and appreciation of spiritual truth and will at a very tender age understand the nature of spiritual warfare. They can profitably be shown how to recognize and overcome the attacks of Satan without fear. Should we really be surprised at all this, when we remember that Jesus said "of such is the Kingdom of God"?

Prayer for the Protection of Children

Father, I entrust my children to you. They are your gifts to me. I ask you to surround _____ with your presence and to shield them from Satan's power. God, shed your light upon your servants; bathe us with the joy of your redemption. Cover _____ with the power of the blood of your Son. I ask you, Father, to expose and destroy schemes of the enemy planned against _____ and to assign your holy angels to guard and protect them, according to your perfect will.

The children of your servants will live in your presence; their descendants will be established before you.   PSALM 102:28

But from everlasting to everlasting the Lord's love is with those who fear him, and his righteousness with their children's children—with those who keep his covenant and remember to obey his precepts.   PSALM 103:17-18

Protecting Our Young People

What is the right response to a teenager who is into such things as heavy metal music, occult or sensual posters, rebellious attitudes, and questionable friends? Violent, destructive powers *are* targeting youth today. Alert Christians are actively battling for the safety and salvation of young people. Be patient and persevering in your prayer, asking especially on a regular basis for the protection of your child.

Establish values and standards at home. You will probably encounter a fight over music, dress, room decor, attitudes, and so on. Hold the line on standards, and trust God to guide you if and when you should be flexible. I would never allow certain posters or record albums into my home. When your children are away, spend time in their rooms inviting the Holy Spirit to fill the place and commanding evil spirits to leave.

Speak matter-of-factly about the dangers of demonic

influence. Try not to use a moralizing, legalistic tone. Say what needs to be said, pray, and trust the Lord to work. Arrange for your children to be exposed to other healthy peer or adult role models. Surviving the crucible of the teen years is a trial for many. Keep the big picture of God's faithfulness in view, and keep showering your children with petitions to God for protection. Stand solidly on the assurances of Psalm 102:28 and 103:17-18 regarding the children of the righteous. Ask God to honor your faith and work according to his Word. When a teen gets into trouble, you may have to admit that you did "too little too late" to model real Christianity. If this happens, entrust yourself and your problem child to the Lord's mercy, and hope and pray for the best outcome.

Prayer for Protection of a Young Person

Jesus, place your hand on _____, shield him/her from the work of the evil one. Restrain him/her from decisions that will bring permanent harm. I apply the power of your blood to this life. Send your holy angels as a guard and to lead _____ back to you. Hear my prayers—preserve and protect my son (or daughter).

But now that you know God—or rather are known by God—how is it that you are turning back to those weak and miserable principles? Do you wish to be enslaved by them all over again?
GALATIANS 4:9

You were running a good race. Who cut in on you and kept you from obeying the truth?
GALATIANS 5:7

Remember this: Whoever turns a sinner away from the error of his way will save him from death and cover over a multitude of sins.
JAMES 5:20

Praying for the Backslidden

I like to reason with backsliders. *Why* did you walk away from Jesus? *What* happened when you dropped out of Bible study? Most often there are specific issues, hurts, unanswered questions, broken relationships, disappointments in a church or a pastor, that provoke one's departure from faith. Engage these people in conversation. Dig out the questions, uncover the root feelings, then trust God for some answers.

The Lord's answer for rebellious Israel was the pain of an oppressor, a breaking of will and pride through a circumstance out of one's control. Paul, remember, delivered Hymenaeus and Alexander over to Satan "to be taught not to blaspheme" (1 Tm 1:20). When normal means fail, drastic means sometimes become necessary.

Let me share a prayer I have often used in this circumstance:

Prayer for Those Weakening in Their Faith

Lord, I bring _____ to you. Only you can know his/her heart. I cannot make _____ change—only you can. I pray you would open up _____ and help him/her see what has made him/her walk away from you. Give me understanding to see those things as well. Holy Spirit, convict _____ of sin and stir up the desire to be right with you. Make _____ sick of sin. Do whatever you need to break his/her will; yet I ask that you would be gentle. Bring an experience into _____'s life to encourage a return to you.

Father, in Jesus' name I subdue the influence of the enemy in _____'s life. I ask you to separate him/her from the lies and enticements of Satan. God, free _____ from this blindness. Shake him/her to his/her senses. Demonstrate the discipline of your love, yet do it in mercy. I praise and thank you for the work you are going to do in _____'s life.

God our Savior ... wants all men to be saved and to come to a knowledge of the truth.　　　　1 TIMOTHY 2:3-4

Praying for the Lost

Can you do spiritual warfare on behalf of unbelievers? In a very real sense, the lost are held hostage to the blinding and binding influence of the evil one. In the parable of the seed and sower, Jesus depicts the demons who rob people of the ability to understand the truth as the "birds of the air" that steal the seed. Hostages do not set themselves free. A rescue is required. How can we cooperate with the Holy Spirit in seeing the bondage of unbelief broken?

Each man and woman makes a choice to seek light or serve self. Apart from the movement of the individual will to seek the grace of God, our prayers cannot and will not wrench someone free from the grip of sin and the power of Satan. But we may still pray in conformity to God's will, who "wants all men to be saved and to come to a knowledge of the truth" (1 Tm 2:4). Peter tells us God is "not wanting anyone to perish, but everyone to come to repentance" (2 Pt 3:9). Doctrinal issues of election and free will aside, I believe we must pray in confidence for the salvation of each person God brings across our path. If this is God's heart, it must be ours as well. Our role is simply to help another say yes to the conviction of the Holy Spirit and the grace of God offered in Christ. We need to peti-

140

tion the Lord for opportunities to share the Word with those for whom we pray. Then we wait, watch, and follow the Spirit's prompting, always being "prepared to give an answer" (1 Pt 3:15) to a seeking soul. The following petition can be prayed as a silent, focused prayer on behalf of the unsaved person. It is most effective to pray this in the presence of the person, even while involved in friendly contact or conversation.

Prayer for Conversion of Unbelievers

Lord, it is your desire that _____ not perish. Holy Spirit, make Jesus known to _____. Stir within this person the desire to seek salvation and convict him/her of sin. Lord, soften any resistance to the truth and plant seeds of the Word in this person's mind and heart. Lord, break his/her will. Make this person desperate. Bring _____ to the end of him-/herself.

Lord, I ask you to break Satan's power in _____'s life. Spirit of Jesus, silence and subdue the voice of the enemy. In the authority of Christ, I weaken any strongholds in _____'s life. Holy Spirit, move in your power to separate from this person the influence of unclean spirits, and stir him/her to repentance. I bind the power of any spirits of confusion and unbelief that blind the mind. Lord, enable him/her to hear your Word with clarity. Send someone to share a word of testimony.

But if you harbor bitter envy and selfish ambition in your hearts, do not boast about it or deny the truth. Such "wisdom" does not come down from heaven but is earthly, unspiritual, of the devil.   JAMES 3:14-15

Get rid of all bitterness, rage and anger, brawling and slander, along with every form of malice.   EPHESIANS 4:31

But if we judged ourselves, we would not come under judgment. When we are judged by the Lord, we are being disciplined so that we will not be condemned with the world.
1 CORINTHIANS 11:31-32

Dealing With Strongholds in the Church

Just as the adversary seeks to gain a foothold of influence in the life of the individual believer, he also tries to gain influence in a church, ministry organization, or missionary endeavor. Whether you are a pastor, missionary, an active lay leader, or simply one of the flock, I challenge you to open your spiritual eyes to see what I'm saying. *You* may even be part of the problem! You may need to take some action to restore blessing.

When will we learn to discern the enemy's subterfuge and act in authority to subdue it? Typically, openings to enemy infiltration trace to unexposed or unresolved "sin in the camp," among either laity or leadership. This results in a departure of the Lord's favor and a cloud of oppression. As accuser and adversary, the devil takes every advantage of the body's disobedience to God's moral law and works to aggravate unresolved sin. The body of Jesus Christ must seek to maintain both moral purity and unity of the Spirit in order to appropriate fully the Lord's protection from the evil one's accusations.

Pray for the Lord's protection over your church and its leaders. Pray especially for areas of vulnerability through the discernment of the Holy Spirit—areas where bitterness, envy, strife, selfishness, misunderstanding, confusion, or temptation may have crept in. Rebuke the work of the enemy and intercede for righteousness in your church body.

For where you have envy and selfish ambition, there you find disorder and every evil practice. JAMES 3:16

Obey your leaders and submit to their authority. They keep watch over you as men who must give an account. Obey them so that their work will be a joy, not a burden, for that would be of no advantage to you. HEBREWS 13:17

For God is not a God of disorder but of peace. 1 CORINTHIANS 14:33

Signs of Oppression in the Church

Look for some observable signs of "spiritual subterfuge" that may indicate enemy oppression. Typically, *sin can be found in the history of the group,* usually at the leadership level. Most often this may involve sexual immorality, prideful ambition, covetousness, or anger. The temptation always surfaces to sweep the problem aside or deal only with its symptoms. Yet until the sin has been dealt with, the overall life of the fellowship will suffer a deadening effect.

Often a breach of trust carries with it a diminished expression of supernatural love. If trust in leadership has been violated in the past, the sheep will tend to suspect the integrity of the current shepherd. People will often feel isolated, guarded, self-protective. A tentativeness in commitment may pervade relationships.

Another common sign is *a cloud of confusion in church affairs,* extreme difficulty in getting God's mind and direction for the church. We can expect this if we understand that God has backed away. He will not tolerate unconfessed sin. Real vision deteriorates into divisive individual opinions about what the community should be doing. In this situation, Satan finds additional entry points.

A *distinct deadness and nonresponsiveness in worship services* is another major indicator of spiritual oppression. Certainly every church experiences an occasional "flat" worship time when the congregation seems to labor under a corporate lethargy. That happens. On other occasions the worship leader or leadership team may be out of step with the Holy Spirit and unwittingly contribute to the deadness. This is normal.

What I am talking about is a demonic heaviness that crushes and quells the worship. Supernatural opposition may be at work to suppress the kind of praise that pleases God and draws forth his presence. Once the people of God come alive to the explosive power of praise, the devil loses his grip.

Pray that your church community will have
"wisdom and revelation so that you may
know [Jesus] better" (Eph 1:17), "to know the
hope" (v. 18) and "his incomparably great
power" (v. 19). The Lord longs for his body to
reflect his love and glory.

Brothers, if someone is caught in a sin, you who are spiritual should restore him gently. But watch yourself, or you also may be tempted. GALATIANS 6:1

If your brother sins against you, go and show him his fault, just between the two of you. If he listens to you, you have won your brother over. But if he will not listen, take one or two others along, so that "every matter may be established by the testimony of two or three witnesses." MATTHEW 18:15-16

Problem People in the Church

In any group under attack I also quite commonly find *a person or persons who inject a dominating spirit into the life of the church or organization.* This can take the form of bitterness, strife, control, or rebellion against authority. Whether demonically empowered or not, certain members can wear down the pastor through outright criticism or backstabbing and spreading of gossip.

Such "problem people" can also appear in the guise of righteous, well-meaning workers who are very involved in service. These members, however, often serve their own agenda rather than the things of God. And when confronted, such individuals are masters of making *you* feel as if *you* are the problem! "How dare you confront *me!*"

When a person in a position of power is not broken and submitted to the Lord's will, he or she may become an

146

instrument of influence for demonic powers. Those in leadership may experience far more than normal discouragement. This kind of battle wears down many pastors and drives them out of the ministry. Such losses can be minimized by better understanding the spiritual warfare dimension of church life.

The gifts of discernment (seeing as God sees) and prophecy (speaking an utterance prompted by the Holy Spirit) are essential to detect and confront these kinds of influences. Those in leadership should listen to warnings from members of the body who have proven abilities of discernment. Confronting and dealing with "problem people" should only be done after much prayer and never alone. Decisive, Spirit-guided authority is required to root out those who control others in the wrong ways. Do be sure your own attitude is right before dealing with the confusing mixture of human sin and demonic influence.

*Pray for "problem people" in your church
and for the leaders and church members
who must confront them. Pray especially
for protection, repentance, and peace.*

The Lord's curse is on the house of the wicked, but he blesses the home of the righteous. PROVERBS 3:33

But thanks be to God, who always leads us in triumphal procession in Christ and through us spreads everywhere the fragrance of the knowledge of him. 2 CORINTHIANS 2:14

Cleansing Places From Evil

Evil spirits can pollute places with their unholy presence. Such demonization usually occurs when mortal
beings commit immoral acts that open the door to the
activity of demons. For example, a house used for the
manufacture or selling of drugs, a place used for prostitu-
tion, or a building used by a fortune-teller or spiritualist
group may invite demons of bondage, deception, violence,
lust, sexual perversion, or familiar spirits of the occult.
Even when the perpetrators have left the scene, evil spirits
may linger, hoping to prey upon unsuspecting newcomers.

When you purchase a used home, lease office space,
rent a house, or spend a night in a hotel room or condo-
minium, you should cleanse that place from the lingering
effects of sin and wickedness. Lest I invite fanaticism here,
let me state a guiding principle: follow the discernings and
promptings of the Spirit.

> *Pray against any evil presence that may*
> *be attached to your home. Consecrate*
> *every part of your home to the Lord.*
> *Invite his holy presence into each room.*
> *Then fill your home with objects and*
> *activities that bring glory to God. "Those*
> *who honor me I will honor" (1 Sm 2:30).*

Choose for yourselves this day whom you will serve.... But as for me and my household, we will serve the Lord.

JOSHUA 24:15

Now, my God, may your eyes be open and your ears attentive to the prayers offered in this place.   2 CHRONICLES 6:40

But the Lord is faithful, and he will strengthen and protect you from the evil one.   2 THESSALONIANS 3:3

Consecrating and Dedicating Your Home to God

Set your home or place of work apart for God's use. Release your rights to your property. Offer the place to God, inviting his presence. Verbal, visible pronouncement is important in declaring this intention. The head of the household should lead in a prayer of dedication (Jos 24:15). Solomon's prayer of dedication of the temple, though lengthy, may serve as another model for this (2 Chr 6). A word for single parent mothers—*you* can take this role for your home and children and establish the Lord's authority over the place he has provided. You may wish to ask your pastor or a friend to perform such a dedication, but be aware that God will honor *your* faith and prayer.

Prayer for Dedication of a Home

Father, I call to you in Jesus' name and in the power of your Holy Spirit. You are the Lord of my life and of this place. I ask that you would search out and bring into the light any unconfessed sin or act of wickedness committed in this place. I apply the blood of Jesus Christ to break the power of enemy spirits attached to this home. Lord, by the power of the cross and the truth of your Word, I ask you to move on my behalf to cleanse this place of all evil.

Lord, fill my home with your holy presence. Use it for your purposes. Set your watching angels at the boundaries of this property to shield and protect us from evil, according to your Word (Jn 17:15; 2 Thes 3:3). I proclaim that the power of the evil one has no place here. Through the name that is above every name, the King of kings and Lord of lords.

I pray that out of his glorious riches he may strengthen you with power through his Spirit in your inner being, so that Christ may dwell in your hearts through faith. And I pray that you, being rooted and established in love, may have power, together with all the saints,... that you may be filled to the measure of all the fullness of God.

EPHESIANS 3:16-19

I urge, then, first of all, that requests, prayers, intercession and thanksgiving be made for everyone—for kings and all those in authority, that we may live peaceful and quiet lives in all godliness and holiness. 1 TIMOTHY 2:1-2

Strategic Warfare

Strategic spiritual warfare is the endeavor of an individual or group of mature believers to move out in the authority of the Word of God, anointed by the Spirit of God, to expose and overthrow the kingdom of darkness, and to advance the kingdom of light significantly. To be successful, we need to wait for the revelation of the Lord's purposes, persist in intercessory prayer, and identify with the heart of God for renewal in the church, redemption of the lost, and the reformation of society.

The primary activity envisioned in strategic warfare is *intercession* before the throne of God, not *interaction* with fallen principalities. We *are not* called to wield laser beams of biblical authority to destroy heavenly strongholds. We *are* called to destroy in the lives of people (Christian and non-Christian) "strongholds,… arguments and every pretension that sets itself up against the knowledge of God" (2 Cor 10:4-5). We are called to reflect the glory of Jesus Christ faithfully through our obedience to his commands.

This important difference in approach produces a profoundly different result. Strategic spiritual warfare means pursuing the presence of Christ and aligning ourselves with his purposes. We are not assigned to launch spiritual "surface-to-air missiles" into the heavenlies or lob gospel-grenades into presumed enemy bunkers. If we get caught up in this kind of "commando mentality," we run the risk of running ahead of the Lord in fleshly zeal. Strategic warfare must originate from a dependent brokenness, must be directed by the Holy Spirit, and must be initiated at the opportune time.

> *Strategic warfare is a powerful means of tearing down invisible forces of wickedness. Yet it is dangerous and not to be undertaken without a clear calling from God and careful spiritual preparation. If God has not called you into this kind of warfare, pray fervently for those he has, and you will have done your part.*

But the fruit of the Spirit is ... kindness.   GALATIANS 5:22

Let your forbearing spirit be known to all men. The Lord is near.   PHILIPPIANS 4:5, NASB

Therefore, as God's chosen people, holy and dearly loved, clothe yourselves with compassion, kindness, humility, gentleness and patience.   COLOSSIANS 3:12

The Power of Kindness in Spiritual Warfare

I've discovered that we can effectively battle darkness without significantly changing our current pattern of living. In recent years I have expanded my spiritual warfare arsenal to include a powerful weapon that has been all but overlooked in the church today. It's the practical, non-threatening weapon that penetrates defenses: *kindness!* Whether you recognize it or not, the kindness that already resides in you is a powerful tool for changing the spiritual state of things in your world.

The kindness I'm talking about is *practical acts of mercy done by followers of Jesus who are inspired by the Holy Spirit to see others through the eyes of God.* Paul writes that "God's kindness leads you to repentance" (Rom 2:4). The Bible seems to distinguish between the divine quality of kindness and the human quality of niceness. In short, if kindness originates in the heart of God, then only Christians have the ability to be kind in the biblical sense of the word.

Paul lists kindness as one of the hallmarks of a person filled with the Spirit of God (see Gal 5:22). Even the *Webster's Dictionary* definition of kindness implies that it's a quality found only in the spiritual realm by describing it as "having a sympathetic, helpful ... forbearing nature."* I find it interesting that the word *forbearance* is used in that definition because Paul exhorts the Philippian believers to let their forbearing spirits be known to all men (see Phil 4:5, NASB). Forbearance is the ability to view and love people as God sees and loves them.

*As you are kind in the name of Jesus
Christ, those you serve open their hearts
to a relationship with God.*

*Merriam-Webster's Collegiate Dictionary, 10th ed. (Springfield, Mass.: Merriam-Webster, 1993).

Follow my example, as I follow the example of Christ.

1 CORINTHIANS 11:1

Therefore, when Christ came into the world, he said, ... "I have come to do your will, O God."   HEBREWS 10:5, 7

The Son can do nothing by himself; he can do only what he sees his Father doing, because whatever the Father does the Son also does.   JOHN 5:19

Great Expectations of God

Our greatest danger as messengers of God's kingdom is becoming overwhelmed with our task. I find it encouraging to reflect on the principles by which Jesus lived—simple truths that gave him confidence to do the assignments of the day, no matter what the circumstances.

Expect God to work. Jesus rose every day to do the will of his Father. Jesus understood that it's God's power that makes all things possible. God was with Jesus as Jesus did God's will. He is with us in exactly the same way. So step out in faith and exercise the authority God has given you.

Expect the Father's power, not yours. Theologians speak of God as being *transcendent;* that is, he stands on the outside of our problems, unaffected by the things that burden us. Though he is with us by the presence of the

Holy Spirit, he is never bogged down, and his authority is constantly available to us.

Notice what God is doing. Jesus allowed his *Father* to set his agenda. He shared one of the secrets to his success when he said, "Whatever the Father does the Son also does" (Jn 5:19). When we are doing what God wants us to do, we can count on him to open a path for us that only he can open.

Recognize your assignment. Jesus understood his specific call and stayed focused on it so that when he died he was able to say, "It is finished." In other words, "Mission accomplished." Many were healed through Jesus' life, and many demons were expelled; but when he said his work was finished there were still people who needed healing. Clearly, Jesus wasn't on this earth to cast out every demon and heal all the sick. He was here to live among us, show us God's love and power, and enable us to be reconciled to God. That was his mission, and once it was accomplished, he returned to the Father.

> When you know what God wants of you,
> you don't need to take responsibility for
> every conceivable assignment. You cannot
> reach everyone. God has an assignment
> in mind that only you can do. Focus on it
> and complete it well.

Let us not become weary in doing good, for at the proper time we will reap a harvest if we do not give up.

GALATIANS 6:9

You need to persevere so that when you have done the will of God, you will receive what he has promised.

HEBREWS 10:36

Be still, and know that I am God.　　　　PSALM 46:10

Out of the most severe trial, their overflowing joy and their extreme poverty welled up in rich generosity. For I testify that they gave as much as they were able, and even beyond their ability.... They gave themselves first to the Lord and then to us in keeping with God's will.　　　2 CORINTHIANS 8:2-5

More Great Expectations of God

Hang in there when the going gets tough. The Bible often speaks of our need to persevere. One of the primary tactics of the enemy is to get Christians to believe that no matter what we do, our actions are futile and useless. The truth is, God is changing the world through us, whether we recognize it or not.

Rest in the strength of God. We live in his strength, not our own. We came to Christ clinging to him for our salvation and for right standing with God. Now we must depend on God's strength as we go forward.

Be available and step out in obedience. Authority came to Jesus in increasing measure as he gave away the kingdom. It is human nature to reason, "When I get well, when I can afford it, when I'm adequately trained, *then* I'll begin to give of myself." That isn't the way Jesus ran things with the apostles. Time and again he sent them to do his bidding with little or no training; yet the results were historic.

Develop the attitude of "whatever, Lord." Be willing to do the next thing God places before you. As you walk in this perspective, the authority and power of God will flow through you and the world will be changed.

Blessed is he who is kind to the needy. PROVERBS 14:21

He has scattered abroad his gifts to the poor, his righteousness endures forever. PSALM 112:9

Mercy triumphs over judgment. JAMES 2:13

Food and the Palm Reader

At our church, we have delivered food to the needy and shut-ins around town for years. One October afternoon, a call for food came in that seemed routine until Doug and Ken arrived at the address. Ken shook his head as he compared the address on the paper to the house number. "It must be correct. Go figure!"

Capturing their full attention was a pink neon sign depicting a palm reader and advertising the services of *Madame Sheila*. Both men had heard a lot about the dangers of the occult and were uncomfortable. Doug's first reaction was, "There is no way we're giving this food from the church to somebody like that!" But since they had already made the trip, they reluctantly went in.

Twelve customers were in the waiting room. Sheila's niece, a single mom, said she had originated the call. "I heard you guys helped anyone who needed food," she said. "I'm out of everything. I didn't know what else to do but call you. It's OK to receive food even if I don't go to your church, isn't it?"

"We give food out to anyone in need, regardless of their faith," Doug answered. "But I can tell you your future looks pretty bleak without Jesus. Before we leave could we pray for you?"

The waiting room clients and Madame Sheila herself watched as Doug and Ken prayed for this young mother in need. Others began requesting prayer, and soon a makeshift prayer circle formed. After some minutes of praying, Doug offered, "Would anyone like to repent and receive Jesus as your Savior?" To his shock, six in the circle nodded their heads yes. He had explained the gospel once, but based on the eagerness of the customers to receive Christ, he figured he must have been unclear in his explanation. After this second presentation of the gospel, eight wanted to receive Christ! So right there in the waiting room of Madame Sheila's place, eight new believers came into God's kingdom.

Christians showing mercy to a palm reader and her customers—a surprising combination? I have found that serving in the name of Jesus Christ is a powerful means of doing spiritual warfare. As a result of practical love shown by Christians, walls of spiritual resistance often come down.

You can tear down walls of darkness by simply meeting practical needs.

And these signs will accompany those who believe: In my name they will drive out demons. MARK 16:17

For the Son of Man came to seek and to save what was lost. LUKE 19:10

Who despises the day of small things? ZECHARIAH 4:10

A Car Wash and Salvation

Recently we were doing servant warfare in our community by washing cars for free and offering to pray for those we served. Like many we encounter, Bob was taken aback when we refused to take money for our services and told him we did this to show God's love in a practical way. In the conversation that followed, we were able to share the gospel with this man and lead him in prayer on the spot to receive Christ.

As we were praying with him, Bob began to make growling sounds, and it became obvious that demonic powers were present. We took him inside our nearby building for further prayer. As we conversed, Bob confided that he'd suffered irrational fears and obsessive thought patterns for years. After about an hour, he emerged with a born-again heart and freedom from his crippling fears.

I would like to have been a mouse in the corner when Bob got home.

"Honey, what took you so long?"

"Well, I was on my way to the hardware store when I stopped for a free car wash some Christians put on to show God's love in a practical way. I ended up giving my life to Christ, and then I had a couple of demons cast out of me. Other than that, it's been a pretty standard Saturday so far."

Bob and his wife, Carol, joined our church the following weekend. They brought their extended family with them and were actively involved for several years before moving out of the area.

A free car wash is a small thing. That small thing opened the door to another small thing: praying for Bob. That prayer led him to open his heart to Christ and to be set free from demonic powers.

God blesses you when you are willing to serve and empowers you as you look beyond yourself to the needs of others.

Promises for Changing

Can a mother forget the baby at her breast and have no compassion on the child she has borne? Though she may forget, I will not forget you! ISAIAH 49:15

Are not five sparrows sold for two pennies? Yet not one of them is forgotten by God. LUKE 12:6

Parking Meters and God's Love

An effective servant warfare project we do at our church takes place every Wednesday at noon when a group of us who work downtown take part of our lunch breaks to feed parking meters. Each volunteer receives a couple of rolls of dimes and a stack of business cards that say, "Your parking meter looked hungry, so we fed it!" On the back of the card is a brief explanation, a map to our location, worship service times, and a phone number.

One of my parking meter team members is Scott, a bright young litigator who works for one of the largest law firms in town. Every Wednesday Scott leaves the world of attorneys, courtrooms, and corporate clients to serve others in small ways. God is using his simple availability to change the world.

A couple of days after a recent parking meter outing with Scott, a note came in the mail from a lady whose life was touched by our simple service. "Today is my birthday," she wrote. "For the first time in my life everybody forgot my birthday. My husband forgot, my children forgot, even my parents forgot ... but God didn't forget me. I'm not a very religious person, but today God got my attention in a big way when you fed my meter. Thank you."

Small things done with great love build bridges into darkened lives. When you step out to do a small thing, God shows up to accomplish a big thing.

*And the prayer offered in faith will make the sick person well;
the Lord will raise him up.* JAMES 5:15

*Jesus told his disciples a parable to show them that they should
always pray and not give up.* LUKE 18:1

*Keep asking, and it shall be given to you; keep seeking, and
you shall find; keep knocking, and it shall be opened to you.*
MATTHEW 7:7, NASB (MARGIN)

"May We Pray for You?"

We often miss the point that we have this purpose in
life: to do God's will. That's why we're not taken
directly to heaven the moment we're saved through
Christ. When we set out to do the will of God, the same
power and authority Jesus demonstrated flow through us.

The members of a Methodist prayer group in Texas are
finding this to be true. As they go door to door throughout their community they simply ask residents, "May we
pray for you?" One family might need prayer for a finan-
cial need. The next person might need physical healing.
Whatever the need, it is lifted up to the Lord. When the
prayers are answered, the people connect the change with
the presence and love of God. Usually it isn't long before
they move toward Christ.

At one home the prayer group knew something was up when the family just looked at each other with a blank stare and said, "Well, you could pray for Sis." The group found Sis lying on a sofa. She was a teenager, but she looked more like a death camp survivor. She was so anorexic she was in danger of losing her life. Her family explained that she'd been in and out of hospitals and clinics but had found nothing that worked to keep her at an adequate weight. The doctors didn't know what else to do.

The prayer team didn't know much about Sis' medical condition, but they did know how to pray. As they prayed that day they saw some response in her. They came back the next day and the next and the next. After two weeks of daily prayer therapy, Sis began to show obvious signs of recovery. During week three, the entire family was convinced of the reality and love of God and they all received Christ. That was three years ago. Sis is in college now and has no symptoms of her former condition.

As you obey your Father and step out to
do his will, the power and authority of
God will come through your life.

For the kingdom of God is not a matter of talk but of power.
1 CORINTHIANS 4:20

Do not be anxious about anything, but in everything, by prayer and petition, with thanksgiving, present your requests to God. And the peace of God, which transcends all understanding, will guard your hearts and your minds in Christ Jesus.
PHILIPPIANS 4:6-7

If your enemy is hungry, give him food to eat; if he is thirsty, give him water to drink. In doing this, you will heap burning coals on his head, and the Lord will reward you.
PROVERBS 25:21-22

Cookies for the Satanist Next Door

My friends Rich and Cindy work in San Francisco as vocalists in an opera company. When they met their new next-door apartment neighbor in the Haight District not long ago, they knew they'd met their match. Shirley seemed nice until she saw the fish symbol on their door and asked, "You two aren't Christians, are you?"

"Yes, we are. Are you a believer, too?"

"I am a believer, but in Satan."

For a moment they thought she was joking, but over the next few weeks Shirley's dark faith became anything but a laughing matter. The next day she began leaving a daily curse on their doorstep. Rich confided in me, "It's a bit intimidating to find animal parts lying on your doorstep every morning."

As servant warriors, they chose not only to pray for themselves and for Shirley, but also to get some weapons ready. They fired up the oven and began to bake choco-late-chip cookies for Shirley. The other neighbors thought it was an odd sight: Shirley putting curses on Rich and Cindy, and Rich and Cindy baking cookies for her.

It wasn't long before Shirley broke emotionally and spiritually. Rich and Cindy received a touching letter in which Shirley shared, "I've never met people like you. If you are what this Jesus stuff is about, I'm interested."

They told me later, "The entire time Shirley was next door, we felt the deep peace of God in spite of her bizarre actions."

Don't be intimidated or put off by those
people God allows to cross your path.
Prayer and love are profoundly effective
even in the face of great odds.

Promises for Changing

Whether you turn to the right or to the left, your ears will hear a voice behind you, saying, "This is the way; walk in it."
ISAIAH 30:21

See, I have placed before you an open door that no one can shut.
REVELATION 3:8

He who sows righteousness reaps a sure reward.
PROVERBS 11:18

Assignments With Eternal Rewards

I never cease to be amazed watching God work. No greater fulfillment can be found this side of heaven than being available for assignments that have eternal reward. I encourage you to incline your heart ever more to hear these whisperings of the Spirit. Commit yourself to watch for and follow through on those divine promptings. God alone can produce fruit that will last forever. Consider the unspeakable joy of meeting someone in eternity who found life in the Son because of your obedience. The following prayer may serve as a guide as you seek to hear the voice of the Lord:

Our World

Lord, with the eyes of my heart, I want to see you more clearly. I incline the ear of my spirit to listen for your words to me. You have promised your Spirit to guide me into all truth and to prompt prayers that please you and bear fruit. Lord, fulfill your promises to your servant. By faith I receive them.

I admit I wrestle with many obstacles—distractions, a mind that wanders, emotions and moods that rise and fall, personal opinions, and a constant battle with busy-ness. Lord, slow me down, lead me into quietness, help me to hear your still small voice that whispers and witnesses to my spirit. Speak to me, Lord Jesus. Help me, Holy Spirit, to separate your thoughts from my thoughts. Show me the person you are wanting to speak to or touch through me. Show me what to pray, what and when to speak, when to serve. Show me your open doors of opportunity. Lord, make me sensitive to you. Cause me to hear and heed your voice to advance the cause of your kingdom. Amen.

APPENDIX

Names and Functions of Common Demons

Demons have names that signify their functions. Thus, most demon names are the names of emotions. A selection of the names you might find in typical clusters follows (see Hammond & Hammond, *Pigs in the Parlor,* for a similar but more complete listing). Note that there is repetition. Also, I have used italics for the names of demons that usually head the group.

Death, suicide, murder

Destruction, violence

Darkness, deceit

Rage, anger, hate

Hate, revenge, murder

Unforgiveness, anger, bitterness, resentment

Rebellion, stubbornness

Rejection, self-rejection, fear of rejection

Fear, terror, torment, fear of ... (for example, rejection, pain, dark, being alone, being outdoors, heights)

Self-rejection, inadequacy, unworthiness, perfectionism

Guilt, shame, embarrassment, sensitivity

Worry, anxiety, worry about ... (for example, future, the impression one makes)

Deceit, lying

Confusion, frustration, forgetfulness

Criticism, condemnation, judgmentalism, faultfinding

Adultery, seduction

Rape, violence
Depression, anger, defeat
Nervousness
Sensitivity, fear
Doubt, unbelief, skepticism
Pride, arrogance, vanity
Perfection, insecurity
Competition, insecurity, pride
Infirmity, sickness (may be a specific disease such as cancer, diabetes, arthritis or the like)
Blasphemy, cursing, mockery

In addition to such "emotion" demons, others encourage compulsions and addictions. These may go by such names as:

Compulsiveness or compulsion
Control, domination, possessiveness
Performance, pleasing others
Intellectualism, need to understand, rationalization
Religiosity, ritualism, doctrinal obsession
Lust, sexual impurity, adultery
Pornography, sexual fantasy
Homosexuality, lesbianism
Masturbation (obsessive)
Alcohol
Drugs
Nicotine
Gluttony
Anorexia
Bulimia
Caffeine

Occult and cult spirits (including those of false religions) are another category. These often can be quite powerful. Some to look for are:

Freemasonry
Christian Science
Scientology
Jehovah's Witness
New Age
Rosicrucianism
Unity
Mormonism
Ouija Board
Horoscope
Witchcraft
Astrology
Fortune Telling
Palmistry
Water Witching
Buddhism and various Buddhist spirits
Islam and various Islamic spirits
Hinduism and various Hindu spirits
Shintoism and various Shinto spirits

Sources

Excerpts on pages 55, 98-103, 126-27 taken from *Angels Dark and Light,* by Gary Kinnaman (Ann Arbor, Mich.: Servant, 1994).

Excerpts on pages 60-65, 136-41, 149-51 taken from *The Believer's Guide to Spiritual Warfare,* by Tom White (Ann Arbor, Mich.: Servant, 1990).

Excerpts on pages 32-33, 39-45, 53, 72-73, 76-77, 81, 87-89, 128-29 taken from *The Bondage Breaker,* by Neil T. Anderson. Copyright 1990 by Harvest House Publishers, Eugene, Oregon 97402. Excerpts used by permission.

Excerpts on pages 48-49, 75, 82-83, 132-33, 144-147, 152-53, 170-71 taken from *Breaking Strongholds,* by Tom White (Ann Arbor, Mich.: Servant, 1993).

Excerpts on pages 10-19, 26-29, 34-38, 46-47, 51, 56-59, 66-67, 78-79, 84-85, 110-19, 172-74 taken from *Defeating Dark Angels,* by Charles Kraft (Ann Arbor, Mich.: Servant, 1992).

Excerpt on pages 20-21 taken from *Healing Damaged Emotions,* by David Seamands (Colorado Springs: ChariotVictor Publishing, 1996). Used by permission.

Excerpts on pages 71 taken from *Search for Freedom,* by Robert McGee (Ann Arbor, Mich.: Servant, 1995).

Excerpts on pages 154-69 taken from *Servant Warfare,* by Steve Sjogren (Ann Arbor, Mich.: Servant, 1996).

Excerpts on pages 22-25, 68-69 taken from *Spiritual Warfare for the Wounded,* by Mark Johnson (Ann Arbor, Mich.: Servant, 1992).

Excerpts on pages 30-31, 91-97, 120-25, 130-31, 134-35 taken from *Spiritual Warfare,* by Michael Harper (Ann Arbor, Mich.: Servant, 1984).